new vegetarian

celia brooks brown

with photography by **philip webb**

new vegetarian

bold and beautiful recipes for every occasion

RYLAND
PETERS
& SMALL

LONDON NEW YORK

Senior Designer Paul Tilby
Commissioning Editor Elsa Petersen-Schepelern
Editor Maddalena Bastianelli
Production Meryl Silbert
Art Director Gabriella Le Grazie
Publishing Director Alison Starling

Food Stylist Celia Brooks Brown
Food Stylist's Assistant Kate Habershon
Stylist Malena Burgess

First published in the USA in 2001
by Ryland Peters & Small
519 Broadway, 5th Floor
New York, NY 10012

www.rylandpeters.com

Text © Celia Brooks Brown 2001
Design and photographs © Ryland Peters & Small 2001

10 9 8 7 6 5 4

ISBN 1 84172 152 2

Printed and bound in China

for Mom

AUTHOR ACKNOWLEDGMENTS

I am deeply grateful to Eric Treuille and the team at Books for Cooks for their infinite
support and encouragement. Huge thanks to Elsa and Maddie for their hard work
and stoic patience. Much heartfelt gratitude to Philip Webb for creating such
vivacious pictures, and to Kate Habershon, Lizzie Harris, Paul Tilby, and Sarah Cuttle
for making the photo shoot such brilliant fun. I extend warm appreciation to all
who participated in my home tastings (and endured a cold, dark barbecue in
February)—Fisher, Ben, Callum, Alex, Sarah, Jessica, James, Sarah W., Tarda,
Mark J., Dom, Julia, Paula, Paulie, and Steve M.—and to my gorgeous husband
Dan for telling it like it is.

Thanks also to Michael van Straten for nutritional advice and The Vegetarian Society
(www.vegsoc.org) for invaluable information.

NOTES

All spoon measurements are level
unless otherwise stated.

All fruits and vegetables should be
washed thoroughly and peeled, unless
otherwise stated. Unwaxed citrus fruits
should be used whenever possible.

Outdoor grills, ovens, and broilers should
be heated to the required temperature
—if using a convection oven, cooking
times should be reduced according to
the manufacturer's instructions.

Asian ingredients are available in
gourmet stores and certain large
supermarkets, as well as Asian stores.

contents

introduction

Welcome to the new era of vegetarian cooking and eating! It's food for a dynamic life through a healthy diet—and food for the sheer enjoyment of it. It's food modeled on ancient world cuisines, as well as fusing the myriad of modern ingredients available to us today.

Every day, more people are deciding to eat less meat or are giving it up altogether. Cooking vegetarian can require a little more creativity than cooking with meat, but that doesn't mean it has to be complicated. This book aims to inspire both the seasoned cook and the novice, too.

New vegetarian cooking and eating is not about finding substitutes for meat, but rather about shifting the focus. Instead of the conventional "meat and two vegetables," meals without meat should be a varied composition of texture, color, and flavor. Imagine a plate of mezze—creamy hummus singing with garlic, olives twinkling like jewels, smoky grilled vegetables, and grains dressed in fresh lemon juice and peppery olive oil—and a warm and soft pocket of pillowy flatbread to scoop it all up. Do you miss the meat?

BEING VEGETARIAN

There are many reasons for being vegetarian and even if you aren't one, you probably know someone who is. Some of the most common reasons for being vegetarian or cutting down on meat are:

- You may want a healthy diet to give you a greater sense of well-being.
- You may boycott meat because you don't agree with the animal husbandry methods used in the meat and poultry industries.
- You may have environmental concerns.
- You may have religious reasons.
- You may, like me, have a natural dislike for, or indifference towards meat.

Whatever the reason, the health benefits are clear. The World Health Organization recommends a diet that is low in saturated animal fats and high in complex carbohydrates, as found in fruits, vegetables, grains, and legumes—typical of many vegetarian diets. Organizations such as the American Dietetic Association claim that vegetarians may be less likely to develop heart disease, high blood pressure, certain forms of cancer, and many other health problems.

All the reasons for living without meat are good ones. Just remember, no one likes a preaching vegetarian. Celebrate being a vegetarian for the positive reasons, and enjoy a life of cooking and eating truly good food.

BUY FRESH, SEASONAL, AND, IF POSSIBLE, ORGANIC

The fruits of the earth are the main elements of vegetarian eating. Everyone has a built-in self-defense mechanism which makes us sensitive to food that might be harmful to us—it smells odd, looks discolored, lacks luster. But foods can deceive us—a bag of perky supermarket salad may look fresh, but why? Why are February greenhouse tomatoes tasteless spheres? Fresh produce is delicate, so it is usually treated—with preservatives, wax, gas, or irradiation—to sustain its long journey to the supermarket shelves. By purchasing food in season and from as local a source as possible—such as farmers' markets—you'll get fresher, purer produce. The impact on the environment will be less too, as thousands of gallons of airline fuel and diesel go into transporting out-of-season produce across vast distances.

The use of toxic pesticides and artificial fertilizers in the intensive farming of crops does increase productivity, and has shaped the evolution of modern agriculture—but this has had unfortunate consequences. Quality and flavor are compromised by rapid production, toxic residues end up in our food, and the environment becomes polluted. The best way to be absolutely certain that your food is safe and additive-free is to buy certified organic ingredients. It means spending a little more money, but it's worth it for flavor, health, and peace of mind.

The issue of genetically modified or GM foods is another concern. Genetic modification involves the insertion of a gene from one species into another. The aim is to make life easier for the producer, but what about the consumer? It is not yet known what the long-term effects of consuming GM foods will be, nor what effect GM will have on the environment. A soybean plant engineered to resist herbicide can then be sprayed liberally with toxic, non-biodegradable chemicals that end up in the food chain—and ultimately on our plates. Buying organic is one way to avoid GM products, and even then there's some risk.

RELAX AND ENJOY!

Remember, ultimately food is fun. If you can spend time shopping and sourcing the best ingredients, it can be hugely rewarding, especially when you come to eat it.

When we get stressed or worried about cooking, it never seems to taste as good. But don't think of cooking as a chore—it can be very relaxing. Read the recipe carefully and, if you think you can make it, try it. As your confidence grows, you'll find that the satisfaction in the end result is much greater than the effort you put in. Eventually you will want to play around with the recipes and add your own special touches. When you see cooking as a creative process, you can use it to express yourself, as a way to enjoy yourself and please others.

Be brave, be adventurous! But bear in mind that some immortally classic combinations, like pesto for example, are not necessarily improved by substituting, say, lemongrass and Roquefort for basil and Parmesan. Within the boundaries of tradition and sound judgement, there is room for individual expression. Your cooking style is based on who you are, and what you like to eat. Interestingly, many professional chefs still cite their mothers as the best cooks they know.

health notes

without meat, what are we missing out on?

When I tell someone I'm a vegetarian, I often get a reaction of concern—"It must be so difficult to make sure you have a balanced diet," or "Isn't it hard to get enough protein?" The truth is that all the nutrients you need are abundant in vegetarian food. It's just important to eat a varied diet and to understand some basic nutrition facts.

PROTEIN

Protein is an essential part of the diet, but by cutting out meat, you're not in danger of being deprived of protein, unless you plan to live on leaves alone! Grains, legumes, eggs, and dairy produce are all good sources of protein. Protein should make up only 15 percent of the diet so, provided your diet is varied, you will get enough. Try not to rely exclusively on cheese and eggs for protein—they're high in saturated fat which is linked to heart disease, and so should be eaten in moderation.

Proteins are made up of amino acids, of which there are 22 in all. The body manufactures most of these, but eight of them have to be acquired from the diet. Meat, fish, eggs, and dairy produce contain all eight (they are "complete proteins"), but soybeans* are the only non-animal complete protein source —one reason why tofu is such a prized vegetarian food. Rice, grains, legumes, and nuts do not contain all eight, but by mixing these foods in the daily diet, for example, rice with beans, or peanut butter with bread, we make up complete proteins. Recent research shows that these complementary proteins do not have to be eaten together, as the body stores the amino acids short-term.

*Recent research suggests that eating large quantities of soy products can be harmful. As with eggs and cheese, it's best eaten in moderation. Fermentation may reduce harmful effects; so fermented soy products such as soy sauce, tempeh, and miso are thought to be safer.

IRON

Iron plays an essential role in the circulatory system. It is used by the body to manufacture haemoglobin in your blood, which carries oxygen from the lungs to all the tissue cells and major organs in your body. Vitamin C, found in fresh fruit and vegetables, increases iron absorption.

Spinach, though it may have worked wonders for Popeye, is not a good source of iron. It does have a high iron content, but this is cancelled out by a high content of oxalic acid that binds with the iron to form an insoluble substance.

OTHER MINERALS

Meat and fish supply other essential minerals, especially calcium, zinc, selenium, and iodine. Happily all are abundant in vegetarian foods.

B VITAMINS

B vitamins are essential for maintaining a healthy digestive and nervous system. Common food sources include yeast, whole-grain cereals, nuts, green vegetables, and legumes.

B12 is the only B vitamin that doesn't occur in plant foods (except seaweed). Only a very small amount is needed for good health and it can be found in eggs and dairy products. If you are a vegan, you should take this vitamin in supplement form, or incorporate B12-enriched foods into the diet.

OTHER VITAMINS

Vitamin D and Vitamin A are common in meat and fish as well as vegetarian foods. We make our own vitamin D when we are exposed to the sun. We get it from dairy products as well. Vitamin D, however, is not present in plant foods, so vegans are advised to take supplements.

Vitamin A is also found in dairy products, but the body also converts beta-carotene, found in orange-fleshed and dark green vegetables, into this essential vitamin.

OTHER ELEMENTS OF A HEALTHY DIET

Carbohydrate, fiber, and fat are also essential to the diet on a daily basis.

The body converts carbohydrate into energy. The two main types of carbohydrate are starches and sugars. Starches are found in plant-based foods such as

rice, bread, potatoes, pasta, cereals, and legumes. The unrefined types, such as whole wheat bread and brown rice, are the most valuable to the body, as they are rich in fiber and B vitamins.

Sugars which occur naturally in fruit and vegetables (as opposed to a jelly doughnut) are valuable energy and fiber sources as well. These foods contain a whole range of other essential nutrients, and should form a major part of everyday eating.

A moderate amount of fat is essential too—vegetable fats tend to be more unsaturated, which is a more healthy type of fat, than animal fats, which tend to be saturated (this includes cheese and eggs).

VEGETARIAN DAILY DIET

Doctors and vegetarian organizations recommend a daily diet for vegetarians which should include:

- 3 or 4 servings of cereals or potatoes
- 4 or 5 servings of fruit and vegetables (though most nutritionists would recommend 5 to 6 servings)
- 2 to 3 servings of legumes, nuts, and seeds
- 2 servings of milk, cheese, eggs, or soy products.

- A small amount of vegetable oil and butter.
- Some yeast extracts, fortified with vitamin B12.

BEING VEGAN

Being a vegan means not consuming any animal by-products of any kind such as eggs, butter and milk—even honey. And it's not just about food. Vegans will not wear leather or anything else derived from animals. There are a surprisingly large number of everyday items which may use animal products as an ingredient or in the manufacturing process, including moisturizers, chewing gum, wine, beer, toothpaste, and laundry detergent.

Vegans can still share the health benefits of a vegetarian diet despite these restrictions. However, it takes a lot more effort and consideration because there is a risk of malnutrition, especially vitamin B12 deficiency.

If you are considering becoming vegan, find out more about veganism first, and seek the advice of a nutritionist or dietician.

the basics

RICE Long grain or short grain, rice is a traditional vegetarian staple and is amazingly convenient. My favorite is basmati, which has a lovely, nutty flavor and cooks in just 10–12 minutes in boiling salted water. Other varieties include white long grain and Thai fragrant rice. Italian risotto rice and Japanese sushi rice are all short grain. Converted rice is also available: the grains have been steam-treated to drive the nutrients back into the grain. Brown rice, also known as wholegrain rice, is not milled (only the husk from the grain is removed). It takes 30–45 minutes to cook, has a nutty flavor and is high in B-vitamins and fiber. Rice should always be measured by volume and not by weight and cooked in twice the volume of liquid.

COUSCOUS Not to be confused with a grain, couscous is in fact a type of wheat pasta. It is delicious cold in salads or served hot with vegetable stews. It is easy to prepare: simply pour boiling water or stock over the couscous to cover, add a pinch of salt, and let stand for 10–15 minutes until the liquid is absorbed. Alternatively, steam or microwave, then add a little butter. Fluff the grains with a fork.

BULGUR Also known as cracked wheat, bulgur is probably best-known for its use in tabbouleh, a famous Lebanese dish. Bulgur is a good source of carbohydrate and will add bulk to vegetable dishes. Prepare in the same way as couscous, but let stand for 30 minutes.

POLENTA (CORNMEAL) Made from corn, which is ground to a fine or coarse meal. It is fabulous with butter and Parmesan cheese, served soft or set and cut into pieces, then pan-grilled or fried. Do not use the variety that takes only 5 minutes to cook or the ready-made polenta that is vacuum-packed. Both lack flavor and nuance. Polenta (uncooked) can used like breadcrumbs to give a crisp, crunchy coating to food (page 50). For cooking instructions for polenta, see page 72.

TOFU Made from soybeans, tofu (bean curd) is the best protein alternative to meat. Because it has no taste, tofu is usually marinated with strong, assertive flavors, such as garlic, ginger, and chiles, and either stir-fried or roasted. There are two types of tofu: silken tofu, which is soft and smooth, used mainly in shakes, cheesecakes, and cakes, and firm tofu, which has a more robust texture, suitable for stir-frying, deep-frying, and roasting. Firm tofu is also available smoked, but it doesn't need to be marinated, although it can taste artificial. Tofu will not keep long: if it smells sour, don't use it. If you don't use all the tofu at once, put the remainder in a bowl, cover with cold water, refrigerate, and use within 2 days, changing the water at least once.

Tempeh is another protein-rich food. Made from fermented soybeans, it has a firm texture, good flavor, and can be fried, sautéed, broiled, or roasted. It is usually available frozen from natural food stores.

EGGPLANT A very versatile vegetable, eggplant can be stuffed, roasted, char-grilled, fried, or added to rice and pasta dishes, stews, and bakes. Sprinkling eggplant with salt is a traditional technique used to draw out any bitter juices. However, if you buy the modern, non-bitter variety you do not need to do this. But if you plan to sauté eggplant in oil, you may want to add a pinch of salt—it firms up the flesh so that less oil will be absorbed. Salt will also make the eggplant crisper. Resist the temptation to add more oil, because some of the already absorbed oil will be released back into the pan as the eggplant cooks.

CHILES The intense fiery heat of chiles comes from capsaicin, a chemical that is present in varying degrees in all parts of the chile. It is strongest in the membranes and the seeds, so take care when seeding chiles. Wash your hands thoroughly afterwards and take particular care not to touch your eyes—capsaicin can sting. (I always wear rubber gloves when handling chiles.) Chiles are used extensively in Thai and Mexican cooking. As a general rule, green chiles are milder than red ones and the smaller the chile, the hotter it is. There are a few exceptions; the habañero and Scotch bonnet are both large, rippled, and lantern-shaped, and often red, yellow, or orange. Both are best avoided unless you really want to hit the ceiling.

OLIVE OIL Try to use the best extra virgin olive oil you can afford. A wildly expensive estate oil may be wasted in cooking—almost good enough to drink, it should be used in the raw for salads and dunking bread. Like wines, olive oils have different characteristics of fruitiness and pepperiness, and what you love is an individual matter.

COOKING WITH WINE A splash of wine is a welcome addition to many recipes. The only rule of thumb is not to add it at the end of cooking, but at the start, to give the alcohol at least a few minutes to evaporate. My favorites are:

- Madeira (from the island bearing its name) is sweet and nutty—keep a bottle by the stove at all times.
- Port is a fortified wine and in cooking it imparts a deep wine flavor and dark color.
- Vermouth isn't the finest of drinks, except as part of a dry martini, though it is the best fortified white wine for risotto. It can be substituted wherever white wine is required, as it doesn't oxidize and can be kept ready and waiting for splashing.
- Slightly less common are the two Japanese rice wines; mirin, a sweet wine for cooking only, and sake. Both, especially in combination, are wonderful in stir-fries and marinades.

BREADCRUMBS Store-bought breadcrumbs taste stale and are generally bad value. Some bakeries will sell you a cheap bag of crumbs, but you can easily make your own by pulverizing stale cubes of bread in the food processor. You can then freeze them in bags. If you haven't got any stale bread, buy a couple of crusty rolls or a small baguette, slice in half, and toast in the oven until crisp. Break into pieces and process in the machine.

basic recipes

vegetable stock

Using homemade vegetable stock creates a depth of flavor in soups and it is well worth going to the trouble of making. In fact, it's no trouble at all—just boil up a pan of water and pop in a quartered onion, sliced celery with leaves, a sliced carrot, some parsley, and salt and simmer for 30 minutes. And there you have it. But you needn't buy vegetables specifically for stock. Always save the water you've used to steam, blanch, or boil vegetables: cool and store in a sealed bag in the freezer and you'll always have some to hand. Alternatively, boil up vegetable off-cuts. Stock options—good and bad—are:

- Especially good: scallion and leek greens (well washed), broccoli and cauliflower stems, celery leaves, fresh pea pods, herb stems, fennel tops, tomato skins.
- Not so good: onion skins, cabbage leaves, potato, bell pepper seeds.

I have to admit I regularly succumb to the convenience of bouillon cubes or granules. Read the label and go organic or without "flavorings" or additives.

beans

Freshly cooked beans do taste better than canned, but not always infinitely superior. While it's hardly back-breaking to throw some dried beans in a bowl of water and leave them overnight, it does require a little forward planning and possibly takes away a little of the spontaneity. So I've given both options in the recipes. If you are using dried beans, remember:

- Lentils DO NOT need soaking, but should be rinsed before cooking.
- Rinse beans first and check for pebbles or imperfect beans.
- Put the beans in a bowl with 3 times their volume of cold water. Leave 12 hours or overnight (in the refrigerator if it's warm in the kitchen).
- Drain off the soaking water and boil the beans in plenty of fresh water. Let them boil furiously for 10 minutes, then add salt. (Adding salt before this will toughen the skins.)
- Skim off any foam that forms on the surface of the water.
- Beans will cook in between 30 minutes and 2 hours, depending on the type of bean and its age.

basic tomato sauce

2 tablespoons olive oil

1 onion, chopped

3 garlic cloves, chopped

16 oz. canned chopped tomatoes

1 teaspoon balsamic vinegar

1 teaspoon sugar

salt and pepper

Heat the oil in a skillet. Add the onion and sauté gently until translucent. Add garlic and sauté until fragrant. Add the remaining ingredients and simmer gently for 15–20 minutes.

Optional extras: 1 chopped serrano chile (added with the onion), a splash of red wine, Madeira, port, or vermouth (added with tomatoes), or fresh torn basil leaves (added in the last minute of cooking).

basic cheese sauce

2 tablespoons butter

2 tablespoons all-purpose flour

1¼ cups milk

1 cup grated sharp-flavored hard cheese such as Cheddar, Monterey Jack, or Gruyère

Melt the butter in a skillet set over a low heat. Sprinkle with the flour. Cook, stirring, for 2 minutes, to burst the starch grains. Meanwhile warm the milk in the microwave or in a separate saucepan. Gradually pour the warmed milk into the flour mixture, stirring constantly. When thickened, stir in the grated cheese and stir until smooth. Serve immediately.

Optional extras: Infuse the milk by simmering it for a few minutes with a bay leaf, half a sliced onion, and a garlic clove.
At the same time as the cheese, add 2 teaspoons Dijon mustard or 2 teaspoons horseradish.

pesto

a large bunch of basil

1 cup pine nuts, lightly toasted in a dry skillet

2 garlic cloves

½ cup grated Parmesan cheese

⅓ cup olive oil

kosher salt and freshly ground black pepper

Put the basil, pine nuts, garlic, and Parmesan in a food processor and blend. Drizzle in the olive oil little by little. Season to taste.

Optional extras: pesto is one of those sublime combinations that really shouldn't be interfered with. An exception is Smoked Chile Pesto, made with chipotle and pimentón—pimentón is smoked paprika, but if you can't find it, use ordinary paprika. Before processing, soak 1 chipotle in hot water, remove the seeds, and chop the flesh. Add to the pesto, with 2 teaspoons mild pimentón, before processing.

basic vinaigrette

It's a matter of personal taste, but I use a ratio of 3 parts olive oil to 1 part balsamic, cider, or wine vinegar. Using a mortar and pestle, mash 1 garlic clove and 1 teaspoon coarse salt to a smooth purée. Whisk in 2 tablespoons vinegar, pepper, and a little sugar. Gradually whisk in 3 tablespoons olive oil until well emulsified.

Alternatively, crush the garlic clove and shake all the ingredients in a screw-top jar.

Optional extras: add 1–2 teaspoons mustard and ½ teaspoon dried herbs de Provence or a small handful of fresh chopped herbs, especially dill. Alternatively, use lemon juice instead of vinegar.

guacamole

2 very ripe avocados

juice of 1 lime

kosher salt or sea salt

Scoop the flesh from the avocados into a bowl. Add lime juice and salt and mash with a fork or potato masher. If made ahead of time, reserve 1 avocado stone and leave it in the guacamole until time to serve. Miraculously, it will stop the guacamole discoloring.

Optional extras: Add 1 crushed garlic clove, 1 chopped chile or a few dashes Tabasco sauce, 1 small, finely chopped onion, 1 chopped tomato, and a small bunch of cilantro, chopped.

the vegetarian pantry

THE FOLLOWING ITEMS, MOST USED IN THIS BOOK, ARE ALL USEFUL TO HAVE ON HAND FOR VEGETARIAN COOKING.

OILS AND VINEGARS

extra virgin olive oil

sunflower oil

sesame oil

truffle oil (drizzle on all things mushroomy just before serving)

white and red wine vinegar

balsamic vinegar

cider vinegar

rice vinegar

sushi vinegar (makes a lovely light salad dressing on its own)

SEASONINGS AND FLAVORINGS

vegetable bouillon cubes or powder

coarse kosher salt or sea salt

fine kosher salt or sea salt (for baking)

Japanese soy sauce, tamari, or shoyu (fermented dark soy sauce)

light soy sauce

Thai sweet chile sauce

Tabasco sauce

chile paste, such as harissa or sambal oelek

vegetarian Worcestershire sauce

tamarind pulp

COOKING WINES

red, white, and Madeira

port (especially ruby port, as it's relatively inexpensive and has a deep color)

vermouth

mirin and sake (see Cooking with Wine, page 11)

NUTS AND SEEDS

sesame seeds

poppy seeds

pumpkin seeds

pine nuts

salted, roasted peanuts

slivered almonds

vacuum-packed chestnuts

PICKLES AND DRIED ITEMS

dried fruits such as raisins, golden raisins, apricots, cranberries, and prunes

pickled onions

capers in salt or vinegar

high-quality olives such as kalamata

pickled jalapeño pepper slices

dried smoked chiles, such as chipotles

dried porcini mushrooms

dried shiitake mushrooms

SPREADS, SAUCES, AND SWEET THINGS

honey

light corn syrup

vanilla extract

rose water

orange blossom water

marmalade

berry, plum, or apricot preserves

lemon or orange curd

peanut butter

unsweetened cocoa powder

vegetarian gelatin alternative

sugar: superfine, soft brown, and confectioner's sugar

BAKING, PASTA, GRAINS, AND LEGUMES

all-purpose flour

bread flour

baking powder

baking soda

wheat germ

masa harina

cornstarch

polenta (cornmeal)

rolled oats

rice: basmati, arborio (for risotto), and sushi rice

bulgur

pasta

couscous

noodles: rice stick, rice vermicelli, egg noodles

flour tortillas

lentils (especially Puy)

dried beans

FOOD IN CANS

refried beans

chickpeas

lima beans

pinto or cannellini beans

corn kernels

coconut milk

coconut cream

peeled plum tomatoes

chopped tomatoes

HERBS AND SPICES

bay leaves

oregano

saffron strands

ground turmeric

mild chili powder (generally a mix with garlic, cumin, and oregano)

cayenne pepper

hot pepper flakes

paprika

pimentón (smoked paprika)

cloves: ground and whole

cinnamon: ground and sticks or bark

whole nutmegs

vanilla beans

cumin: ground and seeds

coriander seeds

cardamom pods

whole fenugreek

sumac (deep red, citrus-flavored spice, excellent sprinkled on salad)

MISCELLANEOUS

mayonnaise

mustard: English, Dijon, wholegrain

creamed horseradish

kitchen equipment

chef's knife and sharpener—buy a large chef's knife. The best are made from high-carbon steel. They have a razor-sharp edge which will need sharpening regularly.

vegetable paring knife

bread knife

food processor with chopping blade, slicing blade and grater.

blender

stick blender (immersion blender) for puréeing soups.

balloon whisk or hand-held mixer

large wok with dome lid—indispensable, not only for stir-frying, but also deep-frying and steaming. Traditional woks, made from iron or carbon steel with a wooden handle (a design perfected over 2000 years ago), are rounded on the bottom, and therefore only suitable for cooking over a gas flame. If your heat source is electric or another fuel, such as oil or wood, opt for a modern version with a partly flat base.

To season a new traditional wok, scrub well, rinse and dry. Wipe with vegetable oil and place over a low flame for 10 minutes. Cool, wipe away the burnt film, and repeat the process until it wipes clean. Never scrub when washing, but wipe clean with hot water and a sponge, and rub with vegetable oil after drying. If the wok does get scrubbed or becomes rusty, simply season again.

wok scoop—a shovel-like implement, ideal for stir-frying.

long tongs

spatula

potato masher

bamboo steamer—can be used in the wok or on top of a pan. These are very cheap and will need replacing every so often, as they absorb flavors.

bamboo or wire strainer or flat slotted spoon

large skillet—either nonstick or well-seasoned cast-iron—about 12 inches diameter.

heavy-bottom saucepans in a variety of sizes.

large heavy-duty stove-top grill pan—if you can find one that fits over two gas burners, so much the better.

large mortar and pestle

muffin pans—I have discovered a remarkable silicon-based rubberized Llorente muffin maker which eliminates the need for greasing. It makes 6 plump muffins that just pop out. Sold in stores such as Wal*Mart; KMart; Bed, Bath, & Beyond; and BJ's—or visit www.directlytoyou.com.

springform cake pan—9- or 10-inch diameter, 3 inches deep (springform pans have removable base and sides).

loaf pan—9 x 5 x 3 inch, standard size.

large and medium baking sheets

power shake

We must eat and drink to "break" the "fast" since last night's dinner. However, many of us don't even wake up hungry, or we're too busy getting ready for work or feeding the family. It's likely we'll put off eating until late morning, when our stomachs rumble loudly and we reach for a delicious but unhealthy sweet pastry. Instead, spare just five minutes in the morning to make a nutritious, filling shake to kick-start your day.

about 1 cup prepared fruit, such as berries, mango, banana, papaya, peach, apricot, melon, or kiwifruit

1 cup low-fat plain yogurt

1 cup fruit juice, such as orange, apple, pineapple, or cranberry

$\frac{1}{2}$ cup slivered almonds

2 tablespoons honey

3–4 tablespoons wheat germ

a pinch of ground cinnamon

SERVES 2

Put all the ingredients in a blender and blend until smooth. Pour into glasses and serve with a straw. This shake will keep in the refrigerator for 2 days.

VARIATIONS

- Use $\frac{1}{2}$ cup silken tofu instead of the almonds.

- Replace the fruit juice with low-fat milk, soy milk, or unsweetened coconut milk.

- Omit the wheat germ and use rolled oats instead.

- Add other flavorings before blending, such as 1 teaspoon pure vanilla extract, a dash of almond extract, or 2 teaspoons grated fresh ginger.

- For a thick shake, add ice cubes before blending.

muffins

Nothing beats a fresh batch of home-baked muffins for an extra-special treat (with butter if you dare) and a cup of steaming coffee or tea. Though they're best eaten hot from the oven, the muffins can be made the night before, cooled, stored in an airtight container, then reheated before serving.

lemon poppy seed muffins

2 cups all-purpose flour

1 teaspoon baking powder

¼ teaspoon salt

3 tablespoons poppy seeds

1 cup sugar

2 eggs, lightly beaten

grated zest of 2 lemons and juice of 1

6 tablespoons butter, melted, or sunflower oil

1 teaspoon pure vanilla extract

½ cup low-fat plain yogurt

a large 6-cup or small 12-cup muffin pan, well greased

MAKES 6 LARGE OR 12 SMALL MUFFINS

Sift the flour and baking powder into a bowl and stir in the salt and poppy seeds. Add the remaining ingredients and fold everything together until just blended; do not beat or overmix. Spoon the batter into the prepared pan and bake in a preheated oven at 350°F for 20–30 minutes, until golden and firm. Let cool in the pan for 10 minutes, then invert onto a wire rack.

VARIATIONS

- Blueberry Muffins: omit the poppy seeds, lemon zest, and juice. Fold 1½ cups blueberries into the batter.

- Fruit and Nut Muffins: omit the poppy seeds, lemon zest, and juice. Add ½ cup dried mixed fruit and ½ cup chopped nuts to the batter.

corn muffins

½ cup all-purpose flour

2 teaspoons baking powder

1 teaspoon salt

2 cups coarse polenta or yellow cornmeal

½ cup sugar

2 eggs, lightly beaten

1 stick butter, melted

¾ cup milk

1 cup fresh corn kernels, or frozen and thawed

a large cup or small 12-cup muffin pan, well greased

MAKES 6 LARGE OR 12 SMALL MUFFINS

Heat the prepared pan in a preheated oven at 375°F for 5 minutes, make the outside of the muffins crisp). Sift the flour and baking powder into a bowl and stir in the salt, polenta or cornmeal, and sugar. Add the eggs, melted butter, and milk and mix until smooth. Add the corn and mix. Spoon the batter into the hot muffin pan and bake at the same temperature for 20–30 minutes, until golden and firm. Let cool in the pan for 10 minutes, then invert onto a wire rack.

VARIATION

- Chile Corn Muffins: reduce the sugar to 1 tablespoon. Add 1 teaspoon chopped serrano chile or 1 cup chopped red bell peppers.

A stack of fluffy, homemade pancakes in the morning will keep you fueled for hours. Make it before bedtime and leave it overnight in the refrigerator. In the morning, you'll have a breakfast feast in minutes.

pancakes

1½ cups all-purpose flour

2 teaspoons baking powder

1 teaspoon salt

3 tablespoons sugar

1 cup milk

2 eggs, lightly beaten

4 tablespoons unsalted butter, melted, plus extra for cooking

MAPLE BUTTER SYRUP

⅓ cup maple syrup

2 tablespoons unsalted butter

MAKES 8–12, SERVES 4

Sift the flour, baking powder, salt, and sugar into a bowl. Mix the milk, eggs, and the 4 tablespoons melted butter in a large pitcher, then add the flour mixture and mix quickly to make a batter (don't worry about lumps—they're good). Alternatively, make the batter in a bowl and transfer to a pitcher.

Heat a cast-iron skillet or flat-surfaced griddle until medium hot, grease lightly with extra butter, and pour in the batter in batches to make rounds, 3–4 inches in diameter. Cook for 1–2 minutes or until bubbles form on top of the pancakes and the underside is golden, then flip each one over and cook for 1 minute. Keep the pancakes warm in the oven while you cook the remaining batches.

Heat the maple syrup and butter together in a small saucepan or microwave, then stack the pancakes on warmed plates and pour over the buttery syrup.

COTTAGE CHEESE PANCAKES

Make the batter as above, then stir in ½ cup of cottage cheese. Proceed with the recipe. Serve with fresh berries, cherry or blackcurrant jelly, and sour cream, crème fraîche, or thick yogurt.

A favorite dish from my home in Colorado. Assembling the burritos is quick and simple, and you can save extra time in the morning if you make the salsa the night before or use a good-quality ready-made salsa—perfect even for the sleepiest of cooks.

breakfast burrito

To make the burritos, put each tortilla on a large sheet of foil, spread with the mashed beans, and top with the cheese. Gather the foil and fold it at the top to seal, keeping the tortilla relatively flat. Put in a preheated oven at 400°F for 7–10 minutes, until the cheese has just melted and the beans and tortilla heated through, but not crisp.

Meanwhile, beat the eggs, milk, chili powder, oregano, salt, and pepper in a bowl. Heat the oil in a nonstick skillet, add the egg mixture, and cook, stirring frequently, until just set. Remove the burritos from the oven, open the foil package, and spoon the scrambled eggs on top. Reseal and keep them warm in the oven.

When ready to eat, unwrap the burritos on a plate and, using the foil to help, roll each one into a cylinder. Top with salsa, guacamole, and a spoonful of yogurt or sour cream.

4 large flour tortillas, 8 inches in diameter

16 oz. canned refried beans, or canned borlotti or pinto beans, rinsed, drained, and mashed

2 cups grated sharp Cheddar cheese

6 eggs

2 tablespoons milk

1 teaspoon mild chili powder

a pinch of dried oregano

1 tablespoon olive oil

kosher salt or sea salt and freshly ground black pepper

TO SERVE

Pickled Jalapeño Salsa or Salsa Fresca (page 62–3)

Guacamole (page 13)

plain yogurt or sour cream

SERVES 4

japanese omelet

This technique for making a very light omelet was shown to me by a Japanese friend. The end result is a delicate *millefeuille*—thin layers of egg, deeply flavored with shiitake mushrooms. This four-person omelet is perfect for brunch or a lazy weekend breakfast. If you are feeling particularly hungry, serve the omelet with broiled vine tomatoes, slices of ripe avocado, and slices of hot buttered toast—bliss.

6 fresh or dried shiitake mushrooms

3 teaspoons vegetable oil

8 eggs

¹/₂ cup vegetable stock or mushroom soaking liquid (see method)

1–1¹/₂ tablespoons light soy sauce

1 tablespoon mirin (Japanese sweet rice wine) or 1 teaspoon sugar

10-inch nonstick skillet

SERVES 4

1 If using dried shiitakes, soak them in hot water for 30 minutes, then drain, reserving ¹/₂ cup of the soaking liquid. Finely slice the mushrooms. Heat 2 teaspoons of the oil in the skillet, add the mushrooms, and sauté for 2 minutes, until golden. Drain on paper towels and set aside.

2 Put the eggs, vegetable stock or mushroom liquid, soy sauce, and mirin or sugar in a pitcher and beat with a fork. Heat the skillet and add the remaining oil. Pour in enough egg mixture to cover the base of the skillet, swirling to coat.

3 Sprinkle with a few mushrooms, then cook until the egg is barely set, but not dry. Using a heatproof, non-metal spatula, loosen the edges and roll up the egg layer from one side of the pan to the other. Do not remove.

4 Pour in more egg mixture as before, letting it touch the rolled omelet. Add a few mushrooms and cook until the egg is barely set. Starting with the cooked omelet, roll it to the other side of the skillet—as you do this the new egg layer with roll up with it.

5 Repeat, layering and rolling until all the mushroom and egg mixture has been used. The finished omelet should be quite thick with many rolled layers.

6 Slide the omelet out of the skillet onto a large sheet of foil. Roll up into a long sausage shape and scrunch the foil at the ends to seal. Let stand 5–10 minutes.

7 Unwrap and remove the foil, then cut the omelet crosswise into 4 or 8 pieces and serve.

celery root, saffron, and orange soup **with parsley gremolata**

An elegant, rich soup, which can also be made dairy-free for vegans—use olive oil instead of butter and leave out the yogurt or crème fraîche. Although the parsley gremolata is optional, it will lift both color and flavor.

Heat the butter or oil in a saucepan, add the onion, and cook until softened. Add the celery root and potato, if using, cover, and cook for 10 minutes, stirring occasionally. Add the remaining ingredients. Bring to a boil and simmer for 20 minutes until the vegetables are tender. Using a hand-held stick immersion blender, purée until smooth. Alternatively, purée in a blender or food processor, in batches if necessary.

To make the gremolata, if using, put all the ingredients in a food processor or spice grinder and process until smooth. Alternatively, use a mortar and pestle.

To serve, ladle the soup into warmed bowls and spoon over the gremolata and sour cream or yogurt.

2 tablespoons butter or olive oil

1 large onion, chopped

1 celery root, about 1½ lb., peeled and cut into cubes (make up the weight with potatoes, if necessary)

4 cups vegetable stock

½ teaspoon saffron strands, lightly ground with a mortar and pestle

1 tablespoon honey

grated zest and juice of 1 large orange

kosher salt or sea salt and freshly ground black pepper

sour cream or plain yogurt, to serve

PARSLEY GREMOLATA (OPTIONAL)

1 garlic clove

1 teaspoon coarse kosher salt or sea salt

a handful of fresh flat-leaf parsley

2 tablespoons olive oil

SERVES 4

soups & salads

I've lost count of how many times I've been told, "this is the best gazpacho I've ever tasted." Ice-cold and enhanced with avocado, lime, cumin, and chile, this soup is refreshingly hard to beat on a hot summer's day. If you have the foresight, freeze cilantro leaves in ice cubes and use them to give your soup a decorative finish.

mexican gazpacho

2 garlic cloves

1 teaspoon coarse kosher salt or sea salt

1 large cucumber, peeled and coarsely chopped

1 yellow bell pepper, seeded and coarsely chopped

2 celery stalks, coarsely chopped

4 ripe tomatoes, coarsely chopped

1 red onion, coarsely chopped

4 cups fresh tomato juice

2 teaspoons cumin seeds, pan-toasted

1 teaspoon mild chili powder

1 ripe avocado, halved and pitted

juice of 2 limes

freshly ground black pepper

TO SERVE

cilantro leaves set in ice cubes, or chopped cilantro

SERVES 6

Using a mortar and pestle, pound the garlic with the salt until puréed. Put the cucumber, bell pepper, celery, tomatoes, and onion in a bowl, add the puréed garlic, and mix well. Transfer half of the mixture to a food processor and pulse until chopped but still slightly chunky. Pour into a bowl. Purée the remaining mixture until smooth, then add to the bowl. Mix in the tomato juice, cumin, chili powder, and freshly ground black pepper to taste.

Chill for several hours until very cold or overnight. If short of time, put the soup in the freezer for 30 minutes to chill.

Cut the avocado into small cubes, toss in the lime juice until well coated, then stir into the gazpacho.

To serve, ladle the soup into chilled bowls, then add a few ice cubes or sprinkle with chopped cilantro.

shiitake and portobello soup

with madeira and thyme

This soup is simplicity itself. There may seem to be a lot of mushrooms in it, but they shrink considerably when cooked and release their flavorful juices into the aromatic broth.

2 tablespoons butter

1 onion, chopped

2 garlic cloves, chopped

10 oz. shiitake mushrooms, torn or chopped into big chunks

10 oz. portobello or other large mushrooms, torn or chopped into big chunks

⅔ cup Madeira wine or dry sherry

2 cups vegetable stock

a bunch of fresh thyme, tied with kitchen twine

kosher salt or sea salt and freshly ground black pepper

TO SERVE

heavy cream

chopped parsley

freshly ground black pepper

SERVES 4

Melt the butter in a large saucepan, add the onion, and cook over a low heat until softened and translucent. Add the garlic, mushrooms, salt, and pepper. Increase the heat, cover, and cook, stirring occasionally, until the mushrooms have softened and their juices released, about 5 minutes.

Pour in the stock and Madeira or sherry and drop in the bundle of thyme. Bring to a boil, then cover and simmer for 15 minutes. Remove the thyme. Using a hand-held stick immersion blender, coarsely purée the mixture. Alternatively, purée in a blender or food processor, in batches if necessary. Ladle into warmed bowls, top with a swirl of cream, chopped parsley, and lots of black pepper, then serve.

lentil, coconut, and wilted spinach soup

Puy lentils are grown in France and have achieved a regal status among pulses. They have a distinctive flavor and, unlike other lentils, hold their shape well when cooked. If unavailable, use green or brown lentils. Add the spinach at the end: it doesn't need cooking.

⅔ cup Puy lentils

4 cups vegetable stock

1 onion, chopped

2 fat garlic cloves, chopped

2 teaspoons ground cumin

1 cup canned coconut milk

2–3 tablespoons dark soy sauce

4 small handfuls of baby spinach, about 2 cups

kosher salt and freshly ground black pepper

SERVES 4

Rinse the lentils, then put in a large saucepan and add enough cold water just to cover. Boil for 10 minutes, then add the remaining ingredients, except the spinach. Reduce the heat and simmer for 20–30 minutes or until the lentils are tender.

Put a small handful of the spinach in 4 warmed bowls and ladle the hot soup on top. The heat from the soup will wilt the leaves. Serve with warm flatbread, such as pita or naan.

This hybrid Thai coleslaw is based on the classic *som tum*, usually made from grated green papaya (when unripe, the fruit is firm, crunchy and perfect for grating). Alas, green papaya is not easy to find, so I've used red cabbage instead. The word "coleslaw" comes from *koolsla*—Dutch for cabbage salad. I merged these two classic dishes to make a salad with a delicious new twist.

thai coleslaw

4 oz. green beans, trimmed

2 cups finely shredded red or white cabbage

3 plum tomatoes, halved lengthwise, seeded, and sliced

4 scallions, sliced

⅓ cup roasted peanuts, coarsely ground

4 cup-shaped lettuce leaves, to serve (optional)

DRESSING

a handful of fresh cilantro

2 red serrano chiles, seeded

2 garlic cloves, chopped

2 tablespoons light soy sauce

2 tablespoons freshly squeezed lime juice

2 tablespoons palm sugar or soft brown sugar

SERVES 4

To make the dressing, reserve a few cilantro leaves, then put the rest in a blender or food processor. Add the chiles, garlic, soy sauce, lime juice, and sugar and blend until smooth. Set aside.

Blanch the beans in boiling water for 2 minutes, then refresh in cold water. Mix the cabbage, beans, tomatoes, and scallions in a bowl. Pour the dressing on top, toss well to coat, and let marinate for about 30 minutes.

Spoon into bowls lined with the lettuce leaves, if using, sprinkle with the ground peanuts and the reserved cilantro leaves, then serve.

grilled asparagus and leaf salad

with sesame-soy dressing

During its short season, I feast on asparagus nearly every day. I think pan-grilling is the best way of cooking the spears—it seals in their sweet, earthy flavor. Turn this salad into a main dish by adding boiled eggs.

3 tablespoons sesame seeds

2 bunches of asparagus, about 24 spears

2 tablespoons dark soy sauce

2 tablespoons balsamic vinegar

5 tablespoons olive oil, plus extra for brushing

2 cups mixed salad leaves, such as arugula, watercress, and spinach

SERVES 4–6

Lightly toast the sesame seeds in a dry skillet, stirring frequently, until golden and popping. Transfer to a bowl and let cool.

Wash the asparagus and cut off any tough stalks. Brush with olive oil. Heat a stove-top grill pan until very hot, add the asparagus (in batches, if necessary) and cook, turning occasionally, until bright green, blistered, and slightly charred, about 5–7 minutes (depending on thickness).

Put the toasted sesame seeds, soy sauce, and balsamic vinegar in a bowl and gradually whisk in the oil until emulsified. To assemble, put the salad leaves on a platter, arrange the asparagus on top, drizzle with the sesame dressing, and serve.

2 lb. new potatoes,
scrubbed

4 scallions, chopped

3 tablespoons capers

½ cup sour cream or
crème fraîche

½ cup low-fat plain
yogurt

1 teaspoon finely grated
lemon zest

½ teaspoon saffron
strands, soaked in
1 teaspoon hot water

kosher salt or sea salt
and freshly ground
black pepper

snipped chives, to serve

SERVES 4–6

Cook the potatoes in boiling salted
water for 15–20 minutes or until tender,
then drain and let cool.

Mix the remaining ingredients in a bowl,
then add the potatoes and turn until
well coated. Cover and chill for at least
30 minutes to let the flavors develop.
Serve sprinkled with snipped chives.

saffron potato salad

No ordinary potato salad: this one is cloaked in
a luscious, creamy dressing flavored with saffron.
Serve it as part of a salad feast: with Puy lentils
dressed in lemon juice, onion, and herbs; and a
green salad tossed in a sweet-and-sour vinaigrette.

1 romaine lettuce, outer
leaves removed, or
2 small lettuce hearts

freshly grated Parmesan
cheese, to serve

CROUTONS

2 thick slices white
bread, cubed

1 tablespoon olive oil

DRESSING

2 eggs

¼ cup freshly grated
Parmesan cheese

3 tablespoons white
wine vinegar

2 teaspoons vegetarian
Worcestershire sauce

1 tablespoon snipped
chives (optional)

¼ cup olive oil

kosher salt or sea salt
and freshly ground
black pepper

SERVES 4–6

This classic salad never seems to lose its appeal and is constantly being updated. The original recipe calls for barely cooked eggs, which many vegetarians find unpalatable and should be avoided if you are pregnant, ill, very young, or elderly. Boiled eggs, cooked until the yolks are just set, make a fantastic dressing, and who needs anchovies when you can use a vegetarian Worcestershire sauce? If unavailable, add an extra pinch of salt instead.

caesar salad

To make the croutons, put the cubes of bread in a bowl, drizzle with the olive oil, and toss until evenly coated. Tip onto a baking sheet and bake in a preheated oven at 375°F until golden and crisp on all sides, about 10 minutes. Check the bread occasionally while cooking, so it doesn't burn. Let cool.

To make the dressing, put the eggs in a saucepan of cold water and bring to a boil. Cook for 5–6 minutes, then drain immediately and cool under cold running water. Peel the eggs when cold, then put in a small bowl and mash with a fork. Add the remaining dressing ingredients, except the oil, and whisk thoroughly. Gradually add the oil—a little at a time—whisking until emulsified.

Tear the lettuce into pieces and put in a large bowl, pour over the dressing, and toss until well coated. Top with the croutons, sprinkle with Parmesan, and serve.

warm chickpea salad

with spiced mushrooms

This entrée salad was inspired by Middle Eastern cuisine, where beans, yogurt, and mint are widely used. Make this dish more substantial by serving it on a bed of couscous or bulgur wheat. The convenience of canned chickpeas may appeal if you don't have time to soak and cook the dried variety. You won't notice any difference in taste.

⅔ **cup dried chickpeas or 16 oz. canned chickpeas**

3 tablespoons olive oil

12 oz. button mushrooms

2 garlic cloves, chopped

1 red serrano chile, seeded and chopped

2 teaspoons ground cumin

juice of 1 lemon

¾ **cup plain yogurt**

a large handful of mint leaves, chopped

8 oz. baby spinach leaves, about 5 cups

kosher salt or sea salt and freshly ground black pepper

SERVES 4

If using dried chickpeas, soak them overnight in cold water, then rinse and drain. Put in a saucepan, cover with water, and bring to a boil. Cook for 10 minutes, then add salt, reduce the heat, and simmer for 1–1½ hours, until tender. If using canned chickpeas, drain, rinse, and drain again.

Heat 2 tablespoons of the oil a skillet. Add the mushrooms, season with salt, and cook until softened. Reduce the heat, then add the garlic, chile, and chickpeas. Sauté for 2 minutes, then add the cumin and half the lemon juice. Cook until the juices in the skillet evaporate, then set aside.

Put the yogurt in a bowl, then add the chopped mint and the remaining lemon juice and oil. Add salt and pepper and mix until blended. Divide the spinach between 4 plates or put on a serving platter, add the chickpea and mushroom mixture, then pour the yogurt dressing over the top and serve.

2 red bell peppers,
halved and seeded

2 yellow bell peppers,
halved and seeded

1 lb. ripe plum tomatoes,
about 4 medium

¼ cup red wine vinegar

2 garlic cloves, crushed
to a paste with coarse
kosher salt or sea salt

freshly ground black
pepper

½ cup extra virgin olive
oil, plus extra for
drizzling

2 tablespoons capers

⅓ cup black olives,
pitted

1 small or ½ large loaf
day-old ciabatta, cut
coarsely into cubes

a bunch of fresh basil,
leaves, torn

SERVES 4–6

Make this sumptuous salad with flavorful, deep-red tomatoes. The bread drinks up the rich, summer flavors of the tomato and roasted pepper dressing. It's important to use a crusty, firm-crumbed bread, such as ciabatta, country-style, or sourdough, so it doesn't revert to a dough-like state.

tuscan panzanella

Put the peppers cut-side down on a baking sheet and broil until blistered and charred. Transfer to a plastic bag, seal, and let cool (the steam will loosen the skin, making it easier to peel). Scrape off the skin, then cut the peppers into strips, reserving any juice.

Halve the tomatoes and scoop out the cores and seeds over a bowl to catch the juice. Purée the cores and seeds in a blender, then press the extra juice through a strainer into the bowl. Discard the pulp and seeds. Cut the tomato halves into strips.

Put the tomato juice, vinegar, garlic, and freshly ground black pepper in a bowl. Gradually add the ½ cup extra virgin olive oil, whisking until blended.

Mix the strips of peppers and tomatoes in a bowl, add the capers, olives, ciabatta, and basil and mix. Add the dressing, toss well to coat, then set aside for 1 hour to develop the flavors. Drizzle with extra olive oil and serve.

To make the latkes, peel the potatoes, then grate on the coarse side of a box grater or in a food processor. Transfer to a strainer and let drain. Press excess moisture out of the potatoes (or they will "spit" when cooked) and put them in a bowl. Finely chop the onion and add to the bowl. Add the lemon zest and juice, flour, baking powder, and salt and mix well. Return to the strainer—liquid will continue to drain out of the mixture while you prepare to cook the latkes.

Heat about ¼-inch depth of olive oil in a skillet. Add rounded tablespoons of the mixture and flatten slightly—don't overcrowd the pan. Sauté for 2–3 minutes on each side until golden and crisp. Remove with a slotted spoon and drain on crumpled paper towels. Keep the latkes warm in the oven while you cook the rest.

To make the avocado crème, scoop the avocado flesh into a bowl and mash with a fork. Add the remaining ingredients and beat until smooth, then serve with the latkes.

NOTE: Latkes make excellent canapés. Sauté teaspoonfuls of the mixture as described above, then serve topped with the avocado crème and cilantro leaves. Makes about 50.

lemon potato latkes

with gingered avocado crème

Though rather indulgent, sautéed potato cakes are worth every wicked mouthful. Keep them small and they'll cook in a matter of minutes. Eat them as soon as possible or reheat later in a very hot oven for 5 minutes. With this spicy avocado accompaniment or one of the dipping sauces on page 59, latkes taste even better.

2 large potatoes, about 1½ lb.

1 small onion

grated zest of 1 lemon

2 teaspoons freshly squeezed lemon juice

¼ cup all-purpose flour

¼ teaspoon baking powder

1 teaspoon kosher salt or sea salt

olive oil, for cooking

GINGERED AVOCADO CRÈME

1 large ripe avocado, halved and pitted

juice of 1 lime

1–2 teaspoons finely grated fresh ginger

½ teaspoon crushed garlic

1 red serrano chile, seeded and finely chopped, or 1 tablespoon chile sauce

1 tablespoon soy sauce

2 tablespoons plain yogurt

MAKES 20–24, SERVES 4

Mix the flour, yeast, and salt in a large bowl and make a well in the center. Add 1 cup warm water and the 2 tablespoons oil. Gradually work in the flour mixture to make a soft but not sticky dough. If it is too dry or too sticky, add extra water or flour, 1 tablespoon at a time.

Invert onto a floured surface and knead thoroughly for 10 minutes, until smooth and elastic. Put in an oiled bowl and turn the dough until shiny all over. Cover with a damp cloth and let rise in a warm place until doubled in size—about 30 minutes.

Meanwhile, to make the topping, cut the onions in half, from top to bottom, and thickly slice lengthwise. Heat the oil in a skillet, add the onions, and sauté until golden. Add the salt, sugar, and wine and cook until the onions have caramelized, about 3–5 minutes.

Sprinkle the polenta or cornmeal onto a baking sheet. This will prevent the focaccia from sticking and will make the base crisp.

Punch down the risen dough with your knuckles, then transfer to the prepared baking sheet and flatten into a round, about 1 inch thick. Top with the caramelized onions and Gruyère. Cover and let rise as before for 30 minutes (no longer or the bread will be hard and dry).

Bake in a preheated oven at 425°F for 30–40 minutes, until golden. Let cool slightly, then cut into wedges and serve.

2½ cups white bread flour

1 teaspoon salt

¼ oz. package active dry yeast*

2 tablespoons olive oil, plus extra for greasing

3 tablespoons polenta or cornmeal

CHEESE AND ONION TOPPING

1 lb. red onions

2 tablespoons olive oil

a large pinch of salt

1 teaspoon sugar

¼ cup white or red wine

1 cup grated Gruyère cheese

SERVES 4–6

To use compressed fresh yeast, crumble ½-oz. into a pitcher, mix to a smooth paste with ¼ cup warm water, then top up to 1 cup. Pour into the well in the flour, then add the 2 tablespoons oil. Proceed with the recipe.

caramelized onion and gruyère

focaccia

For a long time, I was afraid of making bread, thinking it too laborious. Then a few years ago, I made a New Year's resolution to make a loaf twice a week and in doing so overcame my fear. I find that kneading is a good stress-buster. It also keeps my arms in great shape and warms me up on a cold day. This is the simplest of loaves—almost like pizza with a lush topping. It's a meal in itself or is perfect with soup.

An explosion of flavor and texture: the crisp coating protects the deep-fried mushrooms so they are juicy, not greasy. Vary the cheese filling if you can't find dried porcini mushrooms—add a little finely chopped red chile or a mixture of chopped herbs. These balls make a terrific appetizer or delicious party food.

stuffed polenta mushrooms

32 button mushrooms, 1–2 inches diameter

½ cup polenta or cornmeal

3 tablespoons sesame seeds

1 teaspoon salt

2 eggs

sunflower oil, for sautéing

CREAM CHEESE FILLING

⅓ cup dried porcini mushrooms

¾ cup cream cheese

a handful of chives, snipped with kitchen shears

salt and freshly ground black pepper

MAKES 16, SERVES 4–6

To make the filling, pour 2 cups boiling water over the dried porcini and let soak for 20 minutes. Drain (reserving the liquid for another recipe), squeeze dry, and chop finely. Put in a bowl, add the cream cheese, chives, salt, and pepper and mix well. Set aside.

Snap the stems off the mushrooms, then slice ¼ inch off the flat side of each cap. Discard the trimmings. Mound 1–2 teaspoons of the filling into each mushroom and sandwich together to make 16 balls. Make sure the caps fit snugly together.

Mix the polenta or cornmeal, sesame seeds, and salt in a bowl. Break the eggs into a small bowl and beat. Dip 1 ball into the egg, coat well, then roll in the polenta mixture, pressing the mixture onto any uncovered area. Repeat until all the balls have been used. Chill for 15 minutes or until needed.

Heat about 1 inch depth of oil in a large skillet until hot or until a cube of bread browns in 30 seconds. Add the balls and fry for about 10 minutes until lightly golden all over. Remove with a slotted spoon and drain on crumpled paper towels. Serve hot.

large flour tortillas,
8-inch diameter

Cheddar cheese, grated,
feta cheese, crumbled,
or cream cheese

sunflower oil, for
greasing

FILLING, CHOOSE FROM:
chopped tomatoes

chopped scallions

chopped medium-hot
red chiles, such as
serrano

sliced pickled jalapeño
chiles

finely sliced zucchini

sliced mushrooms

chopped bell peppers

chopped avocado

pitted black olives

mashed, canned beans
such as refried, black,
pinto, or borlotti beans

ground cumin

pimentón (smoked
paprika)

TO SERVE (OPTIONAL)
chopped cilantro

plain yogurt, crème
fraîche, or sour cream

**SERVE 1 TORTILLA
PER PERSON**

Lightly grease a large skillet with 1 teaspoon of oil. Lay a tortilla flat in the pan and cover with cheese and 4 or 5 fillings of your choice. Top with a second tortilla and press down gently. Cook over a moderate heat until the bottom tortilla is golden and crisp, about 5–7 minutes. Cover with a plate, turn the pan over, and lift it off. Slide the inverted quesadilla back into the pan and cook as before. Cut into triangles.

Serve with chopped cilantro and yogurt, crème fraîche, or sour cream, if using.

VARIATION

To broil or bake the quesadillas, put a tortilla on a lightly greased baking sheet, top with cheese, preferably Cheddar, and add 4–5 fillings of your choice. Cook under a hot broiler or in a preheated oven at 350°F for 10 minutes or until the cheese is golden.

quesadillas

You're heading for the refrigerator in search of something to demolish your small but acute appetite. You find some tomatoes, scallions, cheese, and a package of flour tortillas—and presto! Your hunger will be satisfied in less than 15 minutes. I haven't given quantities—there's no need, just pile on as much filling as you like. Fried, broiled, or baked, this Mexican snack also makes excellent party food.

topped bruschetta

Bruschetta is a fancy Italian name for toast. But I'm not talking about any old toasted bread—it has to be a crusty, open-textured loaf, such as ciabatta, sourdough, or country-style, rubbed with garlic and drizzled with olive oil. Pile high with either of these juicy toppings and serve 2 pieces per person for a stunning appetizer or 3 for a snack or light lunch.

1 ciabatta loaf or other country-style bread

1 fat garlic clove, halved crosswise

fruity extra virgin olive oil, for drizzling

SLOW-ROASTED TOMATOES

2 lb. plum tomatoes, about 10

3 garlic cloves, sliced

2 tablespoons olive oil

2 teaspoons balsamic vinegar

a pinch of sugar

kosher salt or sea salt and freshly ground black pepper

5–6 basil leaves, torn, to serve (optional)

WILD MUSHROOMS WITH APPLES AND MADEIRA

1 tablespoon butter

8 oz. mixed wild mushrooms, such as chanterelles, porcini, and oysters, or a mixture of wild and cultivated mushrooms, cleaned and sliced if large

1 Granny Smith apple, sliced

1 tablespoon freshly squeezed lemon juice

1/3 cup Madeira wine or dry sherry

1/3 cup mascarpone cheese

kosher salt or sea salt and freshly ground black pepper

chopped parsley, to serve

SERVES 4–6.

To make the bruschetta, cut the bread into slices 1 inch thick. Rub the slices all over, especially the crust, with the cut end of the garlic halves and drizzle with olive oil. Toast, grill, or char-grill until golden and toasted on both sides.

To make the tomato topping, cut the plum tomatoes in half lengthwise and put, cut side up, on a baking sheet lined with foil. Tuck in the garlic and drizzle with the olive oil and balsamic vinegar. Sprinkle with the sugar, salt, and pepper, then roast in a preheated oven at 300°F for 1½–2 hours, until the tomatoes have shrunken slightly and are golden at the edges. To serve, spoon onto the bruschetta and top with basil, if using.

To make the mushroom topping, melt the butter in a skillet, add the mushrooms, salt, and pepper, and cook until softened. Toss the apple slices in the lemon juice, then add to the skillet and sauté for 2–3 minutes. Add the Madeira or sherry and cook, stirring, until the alcohol has evaporated and the sauce has reduced slightly. Stir in the mascarpone until blended. To serve, spoon onto the bruschetta and sprinkle with chopped parsley.

spiced roasted nuts

Liven up a tossed salad or serve as party nibbles with drinks. I'm a great fan of nuts and seeds—my favorites being pumpkin seeds, which puff up impressively when roasted. Rich in iron and minerals, they are good for you, too. Mix your own selection of nuts—choose from sunflower seeds, pine nuts, cashews, macadamia nuts, pecans, Brazil nuts, and almonds.

1 tablespoon olive oil

2 teaspoons dark soy sauce

a squeeze of fresh lemon juice

a pinch of sugar

3–4 drops Tabasco sauce

½ teaspoon paprika

1 teaspoon sesame seeds

1 cup mixed raw nuts and/or seeds

MAKES 1 CUP

Put all the ingredients, except the nuts and/or seeds, in a bowl and whisk until mixed. Add the nuts and/or seeds, stir until coated, then tip onto a baking sheet and spread out in a single layer.

Roast in a preheated oven at 375°F, stirring every 2 minutes, until golden and aromatic.

Let cool, then serve or store in an airtight container until needed.

rarebit

2 tablespoons butter

4 shallots or 1 onion, sliced

1 cup grated Cheddar or Gruyère cheese

⅓ cup beer

a pinch of kosher salt or sea salt

1 teaspoon mustard

2 eggs, lightly beaten

4 slices of bread

freshly ground black pepper

SERVES 2–4

"Welsh rabbit"—also known as rarebit—is a glorified version of cheese on toast. It dates back to the mid-sixteenth century, but over time has evolved into countless variations. If you fancy a comforting snack or something light for brunch, lunch, or supper, this easy-to-make rarebit is hard to beat.

Melt the butter in a heavy-bottom saucepan, add the shallots or onion, and cook until softened. Add the cheese, beer, mustard, and salt. Stir over a low heat until the cheese has melted. Add the beaten eggs and stir until the mixture has thickened slightly, about 2–3 minutes. Don't overcook or you will end up with scrambled eggs. Toast the bread on both sides, then spoon the cheese mixture onto the toast and cook under a hot broiler, until puffed and gold-flecked. Serve with lots of black pepper.

SWEET CHILE SAUCE A great dipping sauce, especially good with wontons (page 114). Put $\frac{1}{3}$ cup light corn syrup, 1 tablespoon soy sauce, and 1 tablespoon rice or cider vinegar in a bowl. Add 1 sliced red serrano chile and mix well. **MAKES ½ CUP**

CHILE COCONUT SAUCE For dipping or dressing stir-fried vegetables. Put $\frac{1}{3}$ cup coconut cream, 2 teaspoons chile paste, and 2 teaspoons freshly squeezed lime juice in a bowl and mix well. **MAKES ½ CUP**

ASIAN VINAIGRETTE Perfect for noodle salads. Put 1 tablespoon dark soy sauce, 1 tablespoon sesame oil, and 1 tablespoon balsamic vinegar in a bowl and mix well. **MAKES 3 TABLESPOONS**

SOY-MAYO DRESSING Divine with potatoes or steamed vegetables. Put $\frac{1}{3}$ cup good-quality mayonnaise in a bowl, add 2 tablespoons dark soy sauce, and mix well. **MAKES ½ CUP**

BLUE CHEESE DRESSING I A thick, creamy dressing for leafy salads. Mash 6 oz. Gorgonzola or dolcelatte cheese in a bowl. Add 3 tablespoons white wine vinegar, ½ cup olive oil, salt, and pepper. Whisk until creamy and smooth. **MAKES 1 CUP**

BLUE CHEESE DRESSING II Superb with Parmesan Patties (page 104) or baked potatoes. Put 6 oz. dolcelatte or Danish Blue and 6 oz. cottage cheese in a bowl. Mash with a fork until blended. **MAKES ABOUT 1 CUP**

super-quick dressings and sauces

Strong flavors will liven up any dish—from raw or steamed vegetables to salads and grilled food. You can serve a selection of these high-speed accompaniments as dips at cocktail parties.

dips, salsas, & sauces

babaganouj

A Middle Eastern eggplant purée. Charring the eggplant over an open flame gives them a subtle smoked flavor. You can also do this on an outdoor grill or in a super-hot oven. If you are oven-roasting, halve the eggplant lengthwise, then score the flesh with a knife, drizzle with olive oil, and roast, cut side up, at 425°F until golden and softened. Peel, then follow the method in the recipe—gorgeous.

2 medium eggplant

juice of 1 lemon

1 garlic clove

2 tablespoons olive oil

2–3 tablespoons plain yogurt

salt and freshly ground black pepper

MAKES ABOUT 2 CUPS

Push a fork into the stem-end of each eggplant and lay them directly over a high gas flame. Rotate the eggplant as the skin chars and blackens and continue to roast until softened, about 15 minutes. Steam will escape when cooked.

Transfer to a plate and let cool. Peel and discard the skin. Don't worry if a few charred bits remain—this will add extra flavor. Put the peeled flesh in a food processor, add the lemon juice, garlic, olive oil, and yogurt, and blend to a purée. Add salt and pepper to taste. Alternatively, crush the garlic and put in a bowl with the peeled eggplant and other ingredients. Mash with a fork until smooth. Check the consistency: if you want a thinner dipping sauce, add more yogurt or oil, as necessary. The texture of the dip will be coarser made this way than by machine.

Serve with toasted pita bread cut into triangles and raw vegetables, such as radishes, carrots, celery, and snowpeas.

sesame yogurt dip

½ cup sesame seeds

½ cup plain yogurt

½ cup mayonnaise

2–3 tablespoons dark soy sauce

MAKES ABOUT 1½ CUPS

Crudités will disappear in no time at all if you serve them with this dip. Use also as a sauce for steamed vegetables or a nutty dressing for salads. For a well-balanced flavor, I like to use half yogurt and half mayonnaise, but you can use all mayonnaise or all yogurt, if you prefer.

Put the sesame seeds in a dry skillet and toast, stirring until lightly browned and beginning to jump around in the pan. Transfer to a bowl and let cool.

Add the yogurt, mayonnaise, and soy sauce and mix well. This dip is best eaten on the day it's made: otherwise the sesame seeds will lose their crunch.

This piquant mixture is a robust accompaniment for Breakfast Burrito (page 24), Haloumi Fajitas (page 82), and Tamales (page 84–6). It's also a splendid party dip. For grilled food, try the corn or mango variation—its sweetness complements the smoky, charred flavors of outdoor cooking.

salsa fresca

Mix all the ingredients in a bowl and set aside for about 30 minutes for the flavors to develop.

MANGO SALSA

Replace the tomatoes with 1½ cups peeled and diced fresh mango. Use chopped mint instead of the cilantro.

CORN SALSA

Instead of tomatoes, use 1½ cups corn kernels, fresh or frozen, cooked in boiling water until tender.

1½ cups ripe tomatoes, finely chopped

1 small red onion, finely chopped

2 green serrano chiles, seeded and finely chopped

juice of 2–3 limes

a small handful of cilantro, finely chopped

kosher salt or sea salt

MAKES 1½ CUPS

pickled jalapeño salsa

OK, so the tomatoes come out of a can and the chiles out of a jar, but this salsa tastes sensationally authentic and has the added benefit of staying fresh and full of flavor for at least a couple of days in the refrigerator.

1½ cups canned chopped plum tomatoes

¼ cup sliced jalapeño peppers in vinegar, drained and coarsely chopped

2 tablespoons jalapeño vinegar from the jar

1 small onion, finely chopped

a handful of cilantro, chopped

kosher salt or sea salt

MAKES 2 CUPS

Drain the tomatoes through a strainer, shaking to remove excess liquid, then discard the juice. Transfer the tomatoes to a bowl, add the remaining ingredients, and stir to mix. Set aside for 30 minutes for the flavors to develop, then serve.

thyme and mushroom gravy

Gravy is usually served with traditional English sausages and mashed potatoes. Vegetarians don't have to miss out on this classic dish as there are now many top-quality alternatives to meat sausages. Cook spicy, organic vegetarian sausages, then pile onto a bed of creamy mashed potatoes and top with gravy. Chase it all down with a glass of chilled beer.

2 tablespoons olive oil

1 onion, sliced

2 teaspoons fresh thyme leaves

1 bay leaf

1 cup coarsely chopped mushrooms

2 tablespoons all-purpose flour

½ cup port or other fortified wine

1 cup vegetable stock

2 tablespoons dark soy sauce

SERVES 4

Heat the oil in a saucepan, add the onion, and sauté until golden. Add the herbs and mushrooms and cook until softened, about 5 minutes. Sprinkle with the flour and cook, stirring, for about 2 minutes. Stir in the port or wine, vegetable stock, and soy sauce and simmer, stirring, until the gravy has thickened slightly, 3–5 minutes. Remove and discard the bay leaf. Pour the gravy into a pitcher and serve.

½ cup dried lima beans, or 16 oz. canned beans

2 large heads of Belgian endive, about 1 lb.

4 tablespoons butter

4 leeks, about 12 oz., sliced into ½-inch pieces, well washed, then drained and patted dry with paper towels

1 cup vegetable stock

1 cup port

2 tablespoons soy sauce

2 teaspoons sugar

4 sprigs of rosemary

1 bay leaf

1 small red serrano chile, seeded and chopped, or ½ teaspoon hot pepper flakes

kosher salt or sea salt and freshly ground black pepper

SMOKED CHEESE MASH

2 lb. Yukon gold potatoes, cut into small, equal pieces, about 1 inch

2 tablespoons butter

½ cup milk

1⅓ cups naturally smoked cheese, such as smoked Cheddar or smoked mozzarella, cut into cubes

kosher salt or sea salt

SERVES 4–6

If using dried lima beans, soak them overnight in cold water, then rinse and drain. Put in a saucepan, cover with water, and bring to a boil. Cook for 10 minutes, then add salt and simmer for 30 minutes, or until tender. Drain. If using canned beans, rinse and drain.

Cut the endive lengthwise into quarters, but don't trim off the base. Melt the butter in a large skillet, add the chicory, and cook, turning occasionally, until golden, about 10 minutes. Add the remaining ingredients, tucking in the rosemary and bay leaf. Bring to a boil, cover, and simmer for 15 minutes. Turn the chicory over, increase the heat, and cook for a further 10 minutes, until the leeks are tender and the gravy has thickened.

Meanwhile, cook the potatoes in salted boiling water for about 20 minutes, or until tender. Drain thoroughly and return to the pan and set it over a low heat for 1 minute to steam dry. Add the butter and milk and mash until smooth. Stir in the smoked cheese, let stand for 2 minutes, then add salt to taste.

Spoon the potatoes onto warmed plates, top with the braised chicory and bean mixture, and serve with the sauce poured over.

braised belgian endive
with beans and smoked cheese mashed potatoes

Belgian endive has a bitterness which some people find unpleasant, but others find addictive. Cooking helps reduce this taste and the flavor is balanced with the slight sweetness of the beans and aromatic gravy. Creamy mashed potatoes make this hearty meal complete.

entrées

roasted teriyaki tofu steaks

with glazed green vegetables

Dark soy sauce, sweet mirin, and dry sake make up the unique flavors of teriyaki. Add fresh or dried shiitake mushrooms to the marinade for a richer flavor. Marinating the tofu in this assertive Japanese sauce also gives it a succulent, delicate character. You can buy ready-made teriyaki sauce, but it only faintly resembles the real thing, so try to make your own— it's very easy and well worth it.

1 lb. fresh firm tofu, cut into 4 pieces

4 fresh or dried shiitake mushrooms (optional)

8 oz. fresh or dried egg noodles

TERIYAKI MARINADE

½ cup dark soy sauce

½ cup mirin (Japanese sweet rice wine)

½ cup sake

1 tablespoon sugar

GLAZED GREEN VEGETABLES

2 tablespoons sunflower oil

2 garlic cloves, finely sliced

1 cup broccoli florets or chopped broccoli rabe

1 leek, white and light green parts finely sliced

8 oz. baby bok choy, quartered lengthwise, or 2 cups chopped spinach leaves

1 fennel bulb, trimmed and finely sliced

2 teaspoons cornstarch mixed with ¼ cup cold water

TO SERVE

2 scallions, finely sliced diagonally

1 tablespoon sesame seeds, toasted in a dry skillet until golden-brown

SERVES 4

To make the marinade, put the soy sauce, mirin, sake, and sugar in a large skillet and heat, stirring until the sugar has dissolved. Add the tofu and mushrooms, if using. Simmer gently for about 15 minutes, turning the tofu over halfway through cooking.

Transfer the tofu steaks to a lightly oiled baking dish or roasting pan. Spoon a little sauce on top and roast in a preheated oven at 425°F for 10 minutes. Keep them warm. Using a slotted spoon, remove the mushrooms from the remaining sauce, squeeze dry, and slice finely. Reserve the sauce.

To make the glazed vegetables, heat a wok until hot, then add the oil. Add the garlic, broccoli, leek, and sliced mushrooms and stir-fry for 2 minutes. Add the bok choy or spinach and fennel. Stir-fry for 2 minutes. Add the reserved sauce and ¼ cup water, stir, cover, and cook for 2 minutes. Push the vegetables to the back of the wok, add the cornstarch mixture to the bubbling juices, and stir until thickened. Mix the vegetables into the sauce. Cook the noodles according to the package instructions, then drain.

To serve, put a nest of noodles on warmed plates and pile on the vegetables. Turn the tofu steaks over and put shiny side up on top of the vegetables. Sprinkle with the scallions and toasted sesame seeds and serve.

piedmontese peppers

with gorgonzola polenta

Elizabeth David first popularized Piedmontese peppers
in her book *Italian Food* in 1954. There is simply no
better way of stuffing peppers. Olives and capers
replace the traditional anchovies,
adding a slight piquancy,
while sweet tomatoes and basil
caramelize slowly in rich garlicky juices.

The hollowed-out peppers make an excellent container
for the filling, acting like a miniature roasting pan. Serve
hot, warm, or cold with broiled blue cheese polenta and
arugula salad.

PIEDMONTESE PEPPERS

2 red bell peppers

2 ripe plum tomatoes, cut into quarters

8 black olives, pitted

1 tablespoon capers

2 garlic cloves, sliced

8 basil leaves, torn

¼ cup olive oil

2 teaspoons balsamic vinegar

kosher salt or sea salt and freshly ground black pepper

GORGONZOLA POLENTA

¾ cup polenta or coarse cornmeal

2 tablespoons butter

2oz. Gorgonzola cheese, cut into small chunks

kosher salt or sea salt (optional)

TO SERVE

arugula leaves

SERVES 2–4

1 Cut each bell pepper in half lengthwise. Do not remove the stems as this will help to keep the peppers' shape. Cut out the seeds and discard.

2 Put the hollowed-out peppers in a roasting pan. Divide the tomatoes, olives, and capers between the pepper halves. Tuck in the garlic slices and torn basil and spoon the oil and vinegar over the top. Season well with salt and pepper. Roast in a preheated oven at 400°F for 30 minutes or until tender and just blackened around the edges.

3 Meanwhile, to make the polenta, put 2 cups water in a heavy-bottom saucepan, add a pinch of salt, and bring to a boil. Reduce the heat to a simmer and sprinkle in the polenta or cornmeal, stirring well with a wooden spoon.

4 Cook, stirring, until the mixture begins to pull away from the sides of the pan, about 15–30 minutes (depending on the quality and type of polenta) or according to the package instructions. The polenta should be thick and lump-free.

5 Add the butter and salt, if needed, and stir well. (Do not overseason the polenta—the cheese is quite salty already.) Add the Gorgonzola and mix thoroughly.

6 Transfer to a shallow tray or wooden board (dampened with water to prevent sticking) and spread into an 8-inch square. Let cool until firm. The polenta can be made several hours ahead or the day before, then cooled and refrigerated until needed.

7 Cut the polenta into 4 squares, put on a nonstick baking sheet and cook under a very hot broiler until the cheese begins to bubble and melt. To serve, transfer the polenta to warmed plates, top with the bell peppers, and serve with arugula.

Pad Thai, probably the best-known of all Thai noodle dishes, takes only 5 minutes to cook. Use thick ribbon-like rice noodles ("rice sticks") for authenticity, or rice vermicelli or egg noodles. Tamarind, commonly used in Asian cooking, has a unique sour flavor, but you can substitute freshly squeezed lime juice.

pad thai noodles

Heat a wok until very hot, then add the oil. Add the eggs and noodles and stir-fry for about 2 minutes, until the eggs are lightly scrambled. Add the remaining ingredients and stir-fry for a further 3–5 minutes, until the noodles are cooked. Divide between 4 warmed bowls and serve sprinkled with the peanuts, scallions, and cilantro.

¼ **cup sunflower oil**

4 eggs, lightly beaten

6 oz. dried thick rice noodles, soaked in warm water for 5 minutes, then drained

3 cups curly kale or other leafy green, tough central core removed and leaves coarsely chopped

¼ **cup tamarind paste or 2 tablespoons freshly squeezed lime juice**

¼ **cup sweet chile sauce**

¼ **cup light soy sauce**

1 cup freshly grated carrot

1 cup bean sprouts, trimmed and rinsed

TO SERVE

⅓ **cup roasted peanuts, chopped**

4 scallions, finely sliced

cilantro leaves

SERVES 4

To make the spice paste, dry-toast the spice seeds in a skillet, shaking until they pop and turn lightly golden. Transfer to a blender or spice grinder, add the remaining ingredients and ⅓ cup water, and grind to a smooth paste. Set aside.

Roast the eggplant directly over a high gas flame until charred and softened, about 15 minutes. Alternatively, roast in a preheated oven at 425°F for about 40 minutes. Let cool, then peel and discard the skin. Don't worry if a few charred bits remain—this will add extra flavor.

Heat the oil or ghee in a large, heavy-based saucepan, add the onion, and cook until softened. Add the spice paste and stir for 2 minutes to release the aromas, then add the pepper, sweet potatoes, zucchini, and chickpeas. Cover and cook, stirring occasionally, for 10 minutes. Add the tomatoes and 1 cup water, then bring to a boil and simmer, uncovered, for about 20 minutes.

Put the peeled eggplant in a blender, add the coconut milk, and pulse to a coarse purée. Add to the pan and bring back to a simmer. Add salt, if necessary. Cook for 10 minutes, then remove from the heat, cover, and let stand for at least 30 minutes or preferably overnight.

Reheat, then serve with rice, cilantro sprigs, yogurt, and mango chutney.

charred eggplant and coconut curry

I wanted to re-create the subtle smoked flavor of Indian dishes cooked in a tandoor oven—and here is the result. Based on a charred, then puréed eggplant, this unusual curry is incredibly good. Don't be put off by the long list of ingredients for the spice paste—it's easy to make and will add a greater depth of flavor. The curry can be made in advance and, in fact, improves by being left overnight so that all the spicy flavors can develop.

1 medium eggplant, about 8 oz.

2 tablespoons vegetable oil or ghee

1 red onion, chopped

1 red bell pepper, chopped

1½ cups peeled and diced sweet potatoes, about 8 oz.

1 medium zucchini, about 8 oz.

16 oz. canned chickpeas, rinsed and drained

16 oz. canned chopped tomatoes

1 cup unsweetened coconut milk

kosher salt or sea salt, to taste

SPICE PASTE

1 tablespoon cumin seeds

1 tablespoon coriander seeds

½ teaspoon cardamom seeds, about 10 pods

½ teaspoon fenugreek seeds

2 inches fresh ginger, peeled and grated

4 garlic cloves

1 teaspoon ground turmeric

1–2 serrano chiles, seeded, or 1 teaspoon hot pepper flakes

1 tomato, quartered

2 teaspoons kosher salt or sea salt

1 teaspoon sugar

TO SERVE

steamed basmati rice

sprigs of cilantro

mango chutney

plain yogurt

SERVES 4–6

pumpkin and tofu laksa

Laksa is a Malaysian curry. It usually consists of rice noodles, crunchy raw vegetables, and fragrant herbs, bathed in a spicy coconut soup. The distinctive perfume of fresh lemongrass and kaffir lime leaves is fundamental to the spice paste and these are available from Asian food stores and markets. If you can't find these aromatics, replace them with grated lime zest and fresh lemon juice, or use a store-bought laksa paste or Thai curry paste instead, but read the label carefully—most contain ground shrimp.

8 oz. peeled, seeded butternut squash or pumpkin, cut into ½-inch cubes

10 oz. tofu, dried with paper towels and cut into 4 triangles

3⅔ cups coconut milk

¼ cup light soy sauce

2 teaspoons sugar

6 oz. rice vermicelli noodles

2½ cups bean sprouts

1 medium tomato, cut into 8 wedges

2 inches cucumber, cut into thin strips

8 sprigs of cilantro

a large handful of mint leaves

2 scallions, chopped

sunflower oil, for sautéing

SPICE PASTE

2 garlic cloves, coarsely chopped

2 red chiles, seeded and coarsely chopped

2 inches fresh ginger, peeled and finely grated

1 small onion

¼ teaspoon ground turmeric

2 stalks lemongrass, sliced

4 kaffir lime leaves, chopped

SERVES 4

1 To make the spice paste, put all the ingredients and 3 tablespoons water in a blender or spice grinder and purée until smooth (add more water, if necessary).

2 Put the squash or pumpkin in a saucepan, then add salt and 2 cups water. Bring to a boil, then simmer for 10 minutes, until the cubes are tender, but still chunky. Drain, reserving the cooking liquid.

3 Heat 1 inch depth of sunflower oil in a wok or skillet. Add the tofu and sauté until golden and crisp all over. Remove with a slotted spoon and drain on crumpled paper towels. Set aside.

4 Heat 2 tablespoons of the oil in a saucepan, add the spice paste, and sauté for 2 minutes to release the aromas. Add the coconut milk, fried tofu, soy sauce, and sugar. Add the reserved pumpkin liquid. Bring to a boil, then simmer for 10 minutes.

5 Meanwhile, put the noodles in a bowl, cover with boiling water, and let soak for 5 minutes. Drain and divide between 4 warmed bowls.

6 Top with the bean sprouts, tomatoes, and cooked squash or pumpkin. Add a piece of sautéed tofu to each bowl.

7 Ladle over the hot coconut soup, top with the cucumber, cilantro, mint, and scallions, then serve.

Fajitas—usually made with beef or chicken—are utterly delicious and can be adapted easily for vegetarians, using haloumi. This firm cheese from Cyprus is unique; it won't melt when fried and develops a delicious crisp crust. Eat the fajitas as soon as you make them; the haloumi loses tenderness if left for too long after cooking. If you can't find this cheese, use tempeh (page 10), found in the frozen section in natural food stores.

haloumi fajitas

To make the marinade, put the garlic and salt in a mortar and crush to a paste with a pestle. Transfer to a bowl, add the remaining ingredients, except the oil, and whisk together. Add the oil in a steady stream, whisking until the mixture has emulsified. Put the haloumi or tempeh in a shallow dish, add enough marinade to cover, and turn until coated. Put the peppers, onions, zucchini, and mushrooms in a bowl, add the remaining marinade, and mix well. Cover both dishes and let marinate in the refrigerator for at least 30 minutes.

Stack the tortillas, wrap in foil, and put in a preheated oven at 300°F for about 15 minutes until warm. Meanwhile, heat a large skillet or wok until very hot, add the marinated vegetables and liquid, and stir-fry until the juices have evaporated and the vegetables are golden and slightly caramelized, about 20 minutes. Transfer to a heatproof dish, cover, and keep it warm in the oven.

Drain the haloumi or tempeh, discarding the marinade. Put the slices in the skillet or wok in a single layer. (If using tempeh, add 3 tablespoons olive oil to the pan.) Cook over a moderate heat for about 10 minutes, turning halfway through cooking, until golden.

Serve the tortillas, vegetables, and cheese separately, so that people can make their own fajitas. To assemble, put a warm tortilla on a plate, add a spoonful of vegetables to one half and top with haloumi or tempeh. Bring the uncovered half of the tortilla up over the filling, then tuck the corners underneath the fajitas. Serve with guacamole, salsa, and lots of sour cream, crème fraîche, or yogurt.

1 lb. haloumi cheese or tempeh, sliced

2 red onions, halved and cut into wedges

1 red bell pepper, seeded and cut into strips

1 yellow bell pepper, seeded and cut into strips

1 green bell pepper, seeded and cut into strips

1 medium or 2 small zucchini, quartered lengthwise and cut into chunks

8 oz. button mushrooms

MARINADE

2 garlic cloves

1 tablespoon coarse kosher salt or sea salt

4 limes, the grated zest of 2 and the juice of all

a handful of fresh cilantro, chopped

1/2 teaspoon dried oregano

1/2 teaspoon hot pepper flakes

1 teaspoon cumin seeds

1 teaspoon sugar

1 tablespoon white wine vinegar

1/2 cup dark rum

1/2 cup olive oil

TO SERVE

8–10 large flour tortillas, 8 inches in diameter

Guacamole (page 13)

Pickled Jalapeño Salsa or Salsa Fresca (pages 62–3)

sour cream, crème fraîche, or plain yogurt

SERVES 4–6

tamales

These simple cornmeal packages originated in ancient Mexico and are often eaten at fiestas and family celebrations. Masa harina—a special type of cornmeal—is used in the filling, then the tamales are wrapped in a corn-husk jacket before being gently steamed. (Banana leaves also make an excellent protective wrap.) The result—light, fluffy mounds.

Blue masa harina is so-called because the corn kernels are actually this color. It has the best corn flavor, but, if you can't find it, use ordinary masa harina or polenta instead. Serve with rice, refried beans, and salsa for a substantial entrée.

1 stick butter

1⅓ cups masa harina, preferably blue* or polenta

a pinch of salt

1 teaspoon baking powder

1 chipotle chile*, soaked in hot water for 20 minutes, then drained, seeded, and chopped (optional)

about ½ cup vegetable stock or water

7 oz. Cheddar cheese or Monterey Jack cheese, cut into 8 blocks, ½ x 2½ inches

8–10 dried corn husks* or 2–3 banana leaves

TO SERVE

canned refried beans

steamed white rice

Salsa Fresca (page 63)

MAKES 8, SERVES 4

* Available from specialist Latin American food stores.

1 Put the butter in a food processor and mix until light and fluffy. Add the masa harina or polenta, salt, baking powder, and chile, if using, and mix. With the machine running, slowly pour in enough stock or water through the feed tube to make a soft dough.

2 Divide the corn dough into 8 pieces and mold each one around a block of cheese until completely enclosed.

3 If using dried corn husks, soak them in boiling water for several minutes until softened, then drain and separate the layers. Wrap the tamales in a layer of husk, covering with extra bits of husk, if necessary.

4 Using thin strips of husk, tie each end of the package close to the filling to look like a Christmas cracker. Repeat until all the tamales are wrapped and tied.

5 If using banana leaves, cut 16 strips, 2½ inches wide. Put a tamale at the bottom of a strip and roll up. Wrap a second strip around the open ends to close.

6 Push a cocktail stick through the middle of the package to secure. Repeat wrapping in banana leaves and securing until all the tamales are made.

7 Put the tamales in a bamboo steamer set over a saucepan of simmering water. Steam for 1 hour. Serve the refried beans, rice, and salsa separately, so people can help themselves and unwrap their own tamales. This is the fun part!

To make the coulis, heat the olive oil in a saucepan, add the garlic and ginger, and sauté until fragrant. Add the tomatoes, vinegar, sugar, and Madeira or sherry and simmer gently for 20–30 minutes, stirring frequently. Add salt and cayenne pepper to taste. Transfer to a blender and purée until smooth. For an extra-smooth consistency, push the purée through a strainer. Set aside.

Put the trimmed spinach in a large saucepan, cover, and heat, stirring occasionally, until just wilted. Drain and let cool. Wring out in a clean cloth, then chop.

Heat the olive oil in the pan, add the onions, mushrooms, coriander, cinnamon, salt, and pepper, and cook until softened and the juices have evaporated. Add the garlic, sauté briefly, then add the chestnuts. Cook for 1–2 minutes, then add the spinach and marmalade and heat through. Season to taste.

Working with 1 sheet of phyllo at a time (keep the rest covered with a damp cloth to stop them drying out), line the prepared cake pan. Press a sheet gently into the sides of the pan and let the edges overhang. Brush with melted butter and slightly overlap with another sheet. Continue to layer and butter the sheets as before, until the pan is completely covered. Spoon in the chestnut mixture and smooth flat. Fold the overhanging phyllo in towards the center and ruffle the top so the phyllo stands in peaks. Brush with butter.

Bake in a preheated oven at 350°F for 30 minutes. Unmold carefully and slide onto a baking sheet. Return to the oven for a further 20 minutes, until golden and crisp all over. Let stand for a few minutes. Reheat the coulis. Using a serrated knife, cut the torte into wedges and serve with the coulis poured over.

chestnut, spinach, and mushroom phyllo torte

with tomato and ginger coulis

A star replacement for turkey at a vegetarian Christmas dinner or special meal—packed with fresh, spicy, rich flavors. The buttery phyllo is light and crisp, but use olive oil if you are cooking for vegans. Ready-cooked, vacuum-packed chestnuts are extremely convenient to use and the filling can be made a day in advance.

4 cups spinach leaves, well washed, with tough stalks removed

2 tablespoons olive oil

2 onions, chopped

2 cups chopped mushrooms

2 teaspoons ground coriander

2 teaspoons ground cinnamon

3 garlic cloves, chopped

1 lb. cooked, peeled chestnuts, chopped

2 heaped tablespoons thick-cut marmalade

5 sheets phyllo pastry, about 11 x 20 inches

4 tablespoons butter, melted

kosher salt or sea salt and freshly ground black pepper

TOMATO AND GINGER COULIS

⅓ cup olive oil

4 garlic cloves, chopped

2 inches fresh ginger, peeled and chopped

2 lb. canned chopped tomatoes

1 tablespoon balsamic vinegar

1 tablespoon dark brown sugar

⅔ cup Madeira wine or dry sherry

kosher salt or sea salt and cayenne pepper

9-inch springform cake pan, brushed with melted butter

SERVES 6–8

1 medium zucchini, about 8 oz., cut lengthwise into ¼-inch slices

⅓ cup olive oil

3 garlic cloves, chopped

16 oz. canned chopped plum tomatoes

½ teaspoon balsamic vinegar

1 teaspoon dark brown sugar

2 handfuls of basil, leaves torn or coarsely chopped

1 cup arborio risotto rice

4 oz. mozzarella cheese, cut into ½-inch cubes

4 oz. Fontina or other mature, hard cheese, cut into ¼-inch cubes

⅔ cup freshly grated Parmesan cheese

¼ cup toasted breadcrumbs

kosher salt or sea salt and freshly ground black pepper

9 x 5 x 3-inch loaf pan, lightly oiled

SERVES 4–6

torta di risotto

with char-grilled zucchini and three cheeses

Heat a stove-top grill pan until very hot. Brush both sides of the zucchini slices with 2 tablespoons of the oil. Add to the pan and sear, turning halfway through cooking, until softened and marked with black stripes. Alternatively, put on an oiled baking sheet, add salt and pepper, and roast in a preheated oven at 400°F for 15–20 minutes until golden.

Heat the remaining oil in a saucepan, add the garlic, and sauté until fragrant. Add the tomatoes, vinegar, sugar, salt, and pepper. Simmer for 10 minutes or until the sauce has thickened slightly. Stir in the basil.

Add the rice to a saucepan of boiling salted water (there is no need to measure the water). Bring back to a boil, then reduce the heat and simmer until the rice is tender, but still firm (al dente), about 10 minutes. Drain.

Add the rice to the tomato sauce and mix well. Stir in the cheeses and add salt and pepper, if necessary.

Sprinkle 2 tablespoons of the breadcrumbs into the prepared loaf pan, tipping the pan from side to side until coated. Spoon in half the rice mixture and smooth flat. Add the zucchini in a single layer, then top with the remaining rice. Smooth flat, pressing down firmly. Sprinkle with the remaining breadcrumbs. (The torta may be refrigerated at this point, then cooked later.)

Bake in a preheated oven at 425°F for 30–40 minutes or until golden and bubbling around the edges. Let stand for 10 minutes. Run a long-bladed, sharp knife between the torta and the pan, then turn out onto a board or platter, tap the pan all over, and lift it off. Cut the torta into slices and serve with a green salad.

Listen to the "oohs" and "aahs" as you present this dish to hungry friends. It's a totally new way of serving risotto—and the secret vegetable layer is so unexpected. I particularly like zucchini, but you can experiment with other vegetables: char-grilled eggplant, peppers, or asparagus are all delicious. Give yourself a head start—make the torta up to a day in advance, chill until needed, then let it reach room temperature before baking.

vegetables on the side

Cut the eggplant lengthwise into quarters and score the flesh with a crisscross pattern. Slice the zucchini in half lengthwise. Cut a thin slice off the bottom of the onions and cut a cross in the top. Split the chiles in half. Leave the garlic whole.

Put all the vegetables, except the tomatoes, cut side up in a roasting pan or dish. Tuck the rosemary and chiles into the onions. Reserve 2 tablespoons of oil and brush the remainder all over the vegetables. Drizzle with the lemon juice and sprinkle with salt and pepper.

Roast in a preheated oven at 400°F for 30 minutes, then brush the tomatoes with the remaining oil and put on top of the half-roasted vegetables. Cook for 15–20 minutes until the vegetables are golden and the tomatoes have split. If using cherry tomatoes, add them after 40 minutes and roast for a further 5–10 minutes.

1 medium eggplant

2 medium zucchini

4 red onions, unpeeled

2 red serrano chiles

1 whole head of garlic, unpeeled

4 plum tomatoes
or 16 cherry tomatoes,
preferably "on the vine"

4 sprigs of rosemary

¾ cup olive oil

juice of ½ lemon

coarse kosher salt or
sea salt and freshly ground
black pepper

SERVES 4

provençal roasted vegetables

Preparation is kept to a minimum and the result is a thing of beauty. Make sure you provide a side plate to put the bits on as people pluck their way through the sweet, juicy vegetables.

minted grilled zucchini

4 medium zucchini, about 2 lb.

2 tablespoons olive oil

4 teaspoons white wine vinegar

a handful of mint, leaves torn

kosher salt or sea salt and freshly ground black pepper

SERVES 4

Perfect for a summer lunch, this Mediterranean recipe and simple char-grilling technique bring out the best in zucchini. They cook to a sensuous texture and absorb the contrasting flavors of the tangy vinegar and fragrant mint.

Trim and discard the ends off the zucchini, then cut the vegetable lengthwise into ribbon-like slices and put in a bowl. Drizzle with the olive oil and, using your hands, gently toss the slices until well coated.

Heat a stove-top grill pan or nonstick skillet until very hot. Add the zucchini ribbons (in batches, if necessary) and cook until softened and marked with black stripes on both sides. Transfer to a shallow dish and drizzle with the vinegar while the zucchini are still warm. Add salt and pepper and let cool.

Pile the zucchini ribbons into a serving bowl, sprinkle with the mint and lots of freshly ground black pepper. Serve.

12 shallots, unpeeled

8 garlic cloves, unpeeled

2 lb. orange-fleshed sweet potatoes, cut into even chunks

1 teaspoon coriander seeds, crushed

2 red serrano chiles

⅓ cup olive oil

kosher salt or sea salt and freshly ground black pepper

SERVES 4

Put the shallots and garlic in a bowl, cover with boiling water, let soak for 30 minutes, then drain and peel. The skins should slip off easily.

Transfer to a roasting pan and add the sweet potatoes, coriander seeds, and whole chiles. Add the olive oil, salt, and pepper and toss well to coat.

Roast in a preheated oven at 400°F for 30 minutes until golden and tender. Shake the pan from time to time during cooking and brush the vegetables with the pan juices.

roasted sweet potatoes

with shallots, garlic, and chiles

Crisp, golden, and bravely flavored is how I like my sweet potatoes. This recipe is for garlic and chile lovers everywhere!

lemon-roasted new potatoes

Potatoes love to be roasted. These zesty little spuds have a crisp tangy exterior and are fluffy inside. Serve with steamed greens or roasted vegetables.

2 lb. baby new potatoes, scrubbed

¼ cup olive oil

2 lemons, grated zest of both and juice of 1

1 teaspoon sugar

kosher salt or sea salt and freshly ground black pepper

SERVES 4

Cook the potatoes in salted boiling water for 5 minutes, drain, then transfer to a roasting pan.

Whisk the olive oil, lemon zest and juice, sugar, salt, and pepper in a bowl, pour over the potatoes and toss well to coat.

Roast in a preheated oven at 375°F for 20–30 minutes, turning and basting frequently with the pan juices, until golden and tender.

chile greens

with garlic crisps

I often have cravings for dark green vegetables—probably because they're rich in iron and vitamin C. The term "greens"—used loosely to describe any leafy green—includes Swiss chard, bok choy, beet greens, spinach, and much more. Many need only brief steaming or stir-frying to retain color, nutrients, and flavor. Remove any tough stalks before cooking.

1 lb. greens (see recipe introduction above)

2 tablespoons olive oil

4 garlic cloves, sliced

1 red serrano chile, seeded and finely sliced

salt and freshly ground black pepper

SERVES 4

Coarsely chop the greens, but if using bok choy, cut lengthwise into wedges. Gently heat the olive oil in a large saucepan. Add the garlic, sauté until golden and crisp, about 2–3 minutes, then remove and set aside. Add the chile to the infused oil in the pan and cook for 1 minute. Tip in the greens—they will splutter, so stand back. Add salt and pepper and mix well. Cover and cook, turning the greens occasionally using tongs, until tender: spring greens will take 5 minutes; Swiss chard, bok choy, and beet greens, about 3 minutes; and spinach about 1–2 minutes.

Transfer to a warmed serving dish and top with the garlic crisps.

VARIATION

For a festive treat, perfect at Christmas, omit the garlic and chile. Sauté ½ cup pine nuts in the oil until golden, then remove and set aside. Add the greens, the grated zest of 1 orange, and 1 teaspoon sugar and cook as described above. Serve with the pine nuts and ½ cup cranberries sprinkled on top.

Turn ordinary vegetables into something fabulous with this gorgeous Thai-flavored sauce. Use it as a marinade here, but also try it as a ketchup—on veggie burgers or on the vegetarian version of a hot dog. The sauce will keep for a week in the refrigerator.

thai-glazed vegetable skewers

Put the Thai barbecue sauce ingredients in a blender or food processor and blend until smooth.

Peel the mango with a sharp knife and stand it upright on a board, narrow end pointing up. Slice off thick cheeks parallel to the stone and cut off strips around the stone. Cut the flesh into equal chunks.

Thread the skewers with the fruit and vegetable chunks, each starting and ending with a lime leaf, if using. Brush the sauce generously over the loaded skewers, then cover and marinate in the refrigerator for at least 30 minutes. Reserve the remaining sauce.

Put on a hot outdoor grill or stove-top grill pan or under a preheated broiler and cook, turning occasionally and basting with the remaining sauce, until tender and lightly charred.

1 large, firm, ripe mango

1 yellow bell pepper, seeded and cut into 10 pieces

2 small red onions, cut into 10 wedges

2 small zucchini, cut into 10 pieces

1–2 limes, cut into 10 slices

10 button mushrooms

1 red bell pepper, seeded and cut into 10 pieces

5 serrano chiles, halved (optional)

20 kaffir lime leaves (optional)

THAI BARBECUE SAUCE

6 tablespoons coconut cream, or 3 tablespoons coconut milk powder mixed with 3 tablespoons water

⅓ cup dark soy sauce

2 tablespoons dark brown sugar

2 tablespoons rice wine vinegar or freshly squeezed lime juice

3 tablespoons tomato purée

3 kaffir lime leaves, chopped

1 stalk lemongrass, finely sliced

1–2 bird's eye chiles, sliced

1 fat garlic clove, sliced

2 tablespoons sunflower oil

10 metal or long bamboo skewers (if bamboo, soak in water for 30 minutes)

MAKES 10

vegetarian grills

feta-stuffed peppers

The stuffing is not cooked, merely heated through and is more like a warm salad than a hot filling. Roasting the peppers on an outdoor grill gives them a unique, smoky flavor and their natural sweetness combines perfectly with the tangy wheat salad.

Put the bulgur wheat in a bowl, cover with boiling water, and let stand for 30 minutes, until the grains are puffed and swollen. Drain, if necessary.

Cut the peppers in half lengthwise and remove and discard the seeds and membranes. Leave the stalk.

Put the remaining ingredients in a bowl, add the soaked bulgur, season with salt and pepper, and mix well. Pile the stuffing into the pepper halves.

Cook on a hot outdoor grill or stove-top grill pan until the peppers are tender and blackened underneath and the stuffing is warmed through. Serve with a crisp, green salad and warmed pita bread.

½ **cup bulgur wheat**

2 red, yellow, or orange bell peppers

6 oz. feta cheese, crumbled

3 handfuls of mixed fresh herbs, such as parsley, mint, dill, basil, and cilantro, chopped

1 garlic clove, crushed

2 teaspoons finely grated fresh ginger

1 tablespoon sumac or 1 tablespoon freshly squeezed lemon juice

2 tablespoons olive oil

kosher salt and freshly ground black pepper

SERVES 4

parmesan patties

Great outdoor food. Kids and grown-ups can't resist burgers and these are no exception. Make in advance to save time, then chill or freeze until needed. Oven-bake rather than grill outdoors for best results. Let's face it, you'll be popping in and out of the kitchen anyway, so these patties will leave space free on the grill for other things.

Heat the oil in a skillet, add the onions, mushrooms, thyme, and salt, and sauté until the onions are softened and golden. Let cool.

Transfer to a food processor, add the cheeses, beans, breadcrumbs, and freshly ground black pepper. Pulse until mixed, then add the soy sauce, wine, mustard, egg, and cornstarch. Process until mixed, but not too smooth.

Using wet hands, shape the mixture into 8 balls, then flatten into 1-inch thick patties. Put on the prepared baking sheet, cover with plastic wrap, and chill until firm. (At this point, you can freeze the patties, then cook from frozen when needed.)

When ready to cook, brush the tops with extra oil and bake in a preheated oven at 425°F for 25 minutes, until golden and crisp (5–10 minutes longer if cooking from frozen).

Cut the rolls in half and toast, grill, or broil lightly on one side, add the patties and your choice of accompaniments, then close up and serve.

1 tablespoon olive oil, plus extra for brushing

2 onions, chopped

4 oz. mushrooms, coarsely chopped

1 teaspoon fresh thyme leaves

½ cup coarsely grated Parmesan cheese

½ cup grated Cheddar cheese

1 cup canned borlotti or pinto beans, rinsed and drained

1 cup fresh breadcrumbs

1 tablespoon soy sauce

2 tablespoons red wine

1 teaspoon Dijon mustard

1 egg, beaten

1 tablespoon cornstarch

8 soft bread rolls

kosher salt or sea salt and freshly ground black pepper

TO SERVE (OPTIONAL)

salad leaves or arugula

sliced tomatoes

sliced red onions

tomato ketchup

mayonnaise

chile sauce

Blue Cheese Dressing II (see page 59)

MAKES ABOUT 8 PATTIES

turkish stuffed eggplant

If one vegetable could sum up Turkish cooking, it would be the eggplant. I discovered this very clever idea for stuffing whole eggplant in a Turkish cookbook and not only is the process ingenious, but it is also great fun. Use long, slender eggplant, which are perfect for hollowing out and stuffing in this way: the plump variety may take too long to cook evenly without burning. Turn the eggplant often on the grill until they are tender and the skin is deeply browned all over.

2 medium eggplant, preferably long and thin

½ cup couscous

3 tablespoons olive oil, plus extra for brushing

2 medium onions, chopped

4 garlic cloves, chopped

1 teaspoon ground cinnamon

1 teaspoon cumin seeds

½ cup pine nuts

6 dates, pitted and chopped

1 tablespoon orange flower water (optional)

a handful of flat-leaf parsley, chopped

1 medium tomato, cut in half

kosher salt or sea salt and freshly ground black pepper

TO SERVE

plain yogurt

lemon wedges

SERVES 4

1 Using a rolling pin, gently beat the eggplant all over without breaking the skin. Massage, rolling them back and forth on a work surface until collapsed and quite flat, about 1 inch thick.

2 Make a shallow cut around the stem-ends of the eggplant, but do not cut through completely. Twist the top, then pull it off—the core should come away too. Scoop out the inside of the eggplants and coarsely chop. Set aside. Sprinkle a little salt inside the cavity, then put the eggplant, cut side down, in a colander over a bowl to drain.

3 To make the filling, put the couscous in a bowl, cover with boiling water, and let soak for 15 minutes. Drain if necessary. Fluff the grains with a fork, then set aside. Heat 2 tablespoons of the olive oil in a skillet, add the onions, chopped eggplant, and salt, and sauté until softened and golden. Add the garlic, cinnamon, and cumin and cook for 2 minutes, until fragrant.

4 Transfer to a bowl. Heat the remaining oil in the skillet and add the pine nuts. Sauté until golden, then add to the mixture, along with the dates, orange flower water, if using, parsley, and couscous. Season with salt and pepper and mix well.

5 Spoon the mixture into the eggplant, pushing it firmly into the cavities (the eggplant should resume their former shape).

6 Push half a tomato into the top of each stuffed eggplant to plug the hole. Brush lightly all over with olive oil.

7 Cook on a hot outdoor grill, turning frequently, until very tender and well browned, about 30 minutes. Slice into thick disks and serve with yogurt and lemon wedges.

NOTE: To cook in the oven, put the eggplant in a roasting pan and pour in ½-inch depth of vegetable stock and 2 tablespoons olive oil. Cover with foil and roast in a preheated oven at 400°F for 30–40 minutes, until very tender.

These grilled mushrooms are very juicy and have a sensational texture. Use tomatoes, mozzarella, and onions that are the same diameter as the mushrooms so they fit snugly into the caps. A luxurious splash of truffle oil intensifies the earthy mushroom flavor.

stuffed flat mushrooms

with mozzarella and truffle oil

4 large portobello mushrooms

olive oil, for brushing

4 teaspoons truffle oil

4 thin onion slices, the same diameter as the mushrooms

6 oz. mozzarella, cut into 4 slices

a handful of basil leaves, 4 whole, the rest finely sliced

4 large tomato slices, the same diameter as the mushrooms

kosher salt or sea salt and freshly ground black pepper

SERVES 4

Cut the stalks out of the mushrooms and discard. Brush the caps with olive oil and put, gill side up, on a plate or tray. Season with salt and pepper and drizzle the truffle oil onto the gills.

Put a slice of onion inside the cavity of each mushroom, then layer with a slice of mozzarella, a leaf of basil, and a slice of tomato. Season with salt and pepper, sprinkle with the finely sliced basil, and drizzle with olive oil.

Cook on a hot outdoor grill for about 15 minutes (without turning), until the mushrooms have softened and shrunk slightly and the cheese has melted. Serve with ciabatta bread.

mushroom and onion marmalade tartlets

A cross between a tartlet and an open sandwich, these no-fuss party tartlets are so simple to make—there's not even any pastry to make or roll out. It doesn't matter how many tartlets I make, there never seems to be enough to go around—everyone keeps coming back for more. Serve hot for best results.

2 tablespoons olive oil

1 large onion, chopped

1½ cups finely chopped or sliced mushrooms

1 tablespoon sugar

leaves from 2–3 sprigs of thyme

12 slices medium-sliced white bread

unsalted butter, for spreading

2½ cups grated Gruyère or mature Cheddar cheese

kosher salt or sea salt and freshly ground black pepper

a 2-inch glass or plain cookie cutter

two nonstick, 12-cup bun pans or shallow muffin pans

MAKES 24

Heat the olive oil in a skillet, add the onions, and saute until softened and lightly golden. Sprinkle the sugar on top and season with salt and pepper. Add the mushrooms and thyme and cook over a high heat until the mushrooms have softened, about 5 minutes.

Using the top of the glass or cookie cutter, stamp out circles from the bread. (The glass flattens the bread at the edges, which will make the tartlets crisper.) Lightly spread butter on one side of each circle, then use to line the pan, butter side down, and press firmly into place.

Put teaspoonfuls of the mushroom mixture in the bread cups and top with the grated cheese. Bake in a preheated oven at 425°F for about 10–15 minutes until golden and bubbling. Serve hot. Alternatively, let cool, then warm through before serving.

party food

spinach and water chestnut wontons

Fried nibbles are always a favorite at parties. These crisp, golden pockets with a light filling, dipped in a sweet, fiery sauce, will be devoured in moments. Wonton wrappers come in two sizes: 3-inch or 4-inch squares, available fresh or frozen from Asian supermarkets. For this recipe, you will need the small ones. As with all fried foods, wontons are best served as soon as they are cooked and do not reheat successfully. However, you can prepare them in advance, cover, and cook at the last minute—they'll be a huge hit.

5 cups fresh spinach leaves,
tough stalks removed

6 canned water chestnuts,
drained and finely chopped

2 teaspoons finely grated
fresh ginger

a pinch of salt

20 small wonton wrappers

1 egg, beaten

cornstarch, for dusting

sunflower oil, for frying

TO SERVE

Sweet Chile Sauce (page 59)

MAKES 20

1 Put the spinach in a large saucepan, cover, and heat, stirring occasionally, until just wilted. Drain, pressing out excess moisture. Let cool, then wring out in a clean cloth until dry. Chop finely, put in a bowl, add the water chestnuts, ginger, and salt, and mix.

2 Take the wonton wrappers out of the plastic bag, but keep them covered as you work to prevent them drying out. Put a wrapper on the work surface, brush the edges with egg and put about 1–2 teaspoons of the spinach mixture in the middle.

3 To shape the wonton, fold in half (with the filling inside) to make a triangle. Press to seal.

4 Bend the wonton into a crescent shape and bring the 2 opposite longest points together. Stick with a little egg. Repeat, filling and shaping, until all the spinach mixture has been used. Refrigerate or freeze any remaining wrappers.

5 Transfer the wontons to a plate dusted with cornstarch, turn gently until lightly coated, then shake off any excess cornstarch. (This will stop the wontons sticking together).

6 Fill a wok or large saucepan one-third full of oil and heat to 375°F. To test, drop in a piece of wonton wrapper—it will puff up immediately when the oil is at the right temperature. Add the wontons in batches of 5–6 and cook for 1–2 minutes, turning once, until puffed and golden.

7 Remove with a slotted spoon or large straining spoon and drain on crumpled paper towels. Serve hot with Sweet Chile Sauce for dipping.

mozzarella and cherry tomato skewers

A classic mix of Italian colors and flavors—in miniature. Bocconcini (meaning "little bites") are tiny balls of mozzarella. They're perfect for these skewers, but, if you can't find them, use regular mozzarella instead and cut it into 20 cubes. Choose the best olives you can find—marinated if possible.

10 cherry tomatoes, halved

20 basil leaves

10 bocconcini balls, halved, or 6 oz. regular mozzarella, cubed

20 black olives, pitted

olive oil for drizzling

kosher salt or sea salt and freshly ground black pepper

20 toothpicks

MAKES 20

Thread the tomato halves, basil leaves, bocconcini or mozzarella cubes, and olives onto the toothpicks. Lightly drizzle olive oil over the loaded skewers and season with salt and lots of black pepper. Serve.

feta and cumin phyllo packages

3 sheets phyllo pastry, about 11 x 18 inches

4 tablespoons unsalted butter, melted

FILLING

1 tablespoon cumin seeds

6 oz. feta cheese, finely crumbled

a handful of mint leaves, finely chopped

finely grated zest of 1 lemon

baking sheet, lightly greased

MAKES 24

Flaky, bite-size packages are quick and simple to make. Feta cheese is quite salty, so you won't need additional seasoning in these savories—only lots of cool drinks to quench your thirst. Serve Chile Coconut Sauce (page 59) for dipping.

To make the filling, dry-toast the cumin seeds in a skillet until fragrant and lightly golden. Put in a bowl, add the feta, mint, and lemon zest and mix well.

Put 1 sheet of pastry on a work surface (keep the rest covered with a damp cloth to stop them drying out) and brush with a little melted butter. Lay a second sheet on top and brush with more butter. Repeat with the final sheet.

Cut into 24 squares, about 3 inches. Put 1 teaspoon of the filling in the middle of each square, then bring the 4 corners to the center and press along the seams to seal. Dab with melted butter and cover with plastic wrap until ready to bake.

Put the phyllo parcels on the prepared baking sheet and bake in a preheated oven at 400°F for about 10 minutes, until golden. Serve warm or cold.

5 quail eggs
or 2 hen eggs

2 small heads of
Belgian endive

½ cup bean sprouts

¼ red bell pepper, finely
sliced lengthwise into
2-inch strips

½ cup finely sliced red
cabbage

1 scallion, finely sliced
lengthwise into 2-inch
strips

1 baby cucumber,
unpeeled, finely sliced
into strips

20 cilantro leaves

GADO-GADO DRESSING

⅓ cup smooth peanut
butter

1 tablespoon sweet
chile sauce

2 tablespoons dark
soy sauce

MAKES 20

Crisp salad leaves, such as Belgian endive and mini romaine lettuces, make wonderful edible scoops. Filled with a classic Indonesian salad, these leaf cups are a refreshing and colorful addition to any party menu. Quail eggs might have been specially invented for finger food, although they can be difficult to peel. If you can't find them, top the salad with finely chopped hard-cooked egg instead.

gado-gado salad
in Belgian endive leaves

To make the dressing, put the peanut butter in a bowl, add 2 tablespoons boiling water and, using a fork, mix quickly until the mixture is completely smooth. Stir in the chile sauce and soy sauce.

Put the eggs in a small saucepan of cold water and bring to a boil. Simmer for 3 minutes for quail eggs and 7 minutes for hen eggs. Drain immediately and cool under cold running water. Peel, then cut into quarters if using quail eggs, or chop finely if using hen eggs.

Trim the endive and separate into 20 leaves. To assemble, fill the leaves with the bean sprouts and strips of each vegetable. Using a teaspoon, drizzle the gado-gado sauce over the top, then add the cilantro leaves and quail egg quarters or chopped egg and serve.

NOTE: If you are cooking for large numbers, it may be easier and quicker to pipe the dressing over the salad. Use a piping bag fitted with ⅛-inch plain nozzle or plastic sandwich bag with the tip of a corner snipped off.

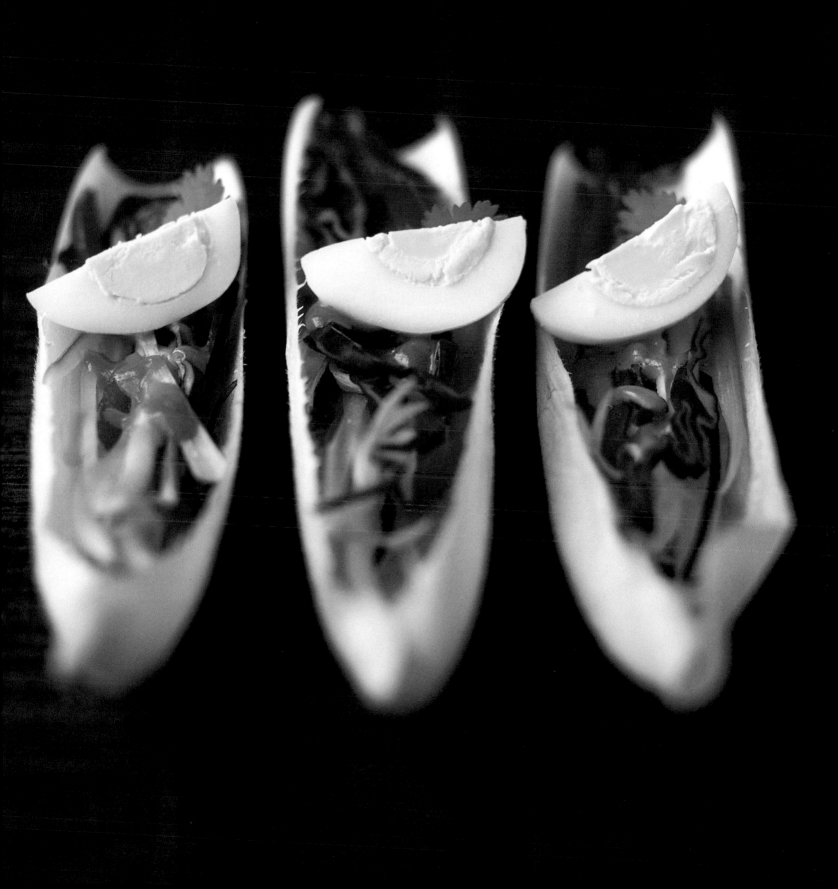

vegetarian sushi roll

Making sushi might require skill and practice, but simple
rolled sushi is very straightforward. This vegetarian
version (minus the raw fish) is a stunning canapé,
appetizer, or even a meal in itself. It's important to use
sushi rice, which cooks to the right sticky consistency.
Serve with traditional Japanese accompaniments:
sweet, pink pickled ginger and a little dish of soy sauce
for dipping. Don't forget the hot green wasabi paste,

but warn people that only a tiny
amount is needed for that fiery
horseradish sensation.

1 cup sushi rice

2–3 tablespoons Japanese rice vinegar or sushi vinegar

a pinch of salt

1 tablespoon mirin (Japanese sweet rice wine) (optional)

3–4 sheets nori seaweed

¼ firm ripe avocado, halved, pitted, and cut lengthwise into thin strips and brushed lightly with lemon juice

1 small cucumber, about 4 inches long, seeded and cut into long thin strips

½ red bell pepper, seeded and cut lengthwise into thin strips

toasted sesame seeds

TO SERVE

Japanese soy sauce

wasabi paste (hot green horseradish)

pink pickled ginger

a sushi rolling mat or heavy-duty foil

MAKES 20–30 PIECES

1 Put the rice in a strainer and wash well under cold running water until the water runs clear. Drain, let stand for at least 30 minutes, then transfer to a heavy-bottom saucepan.

2 Pour in enough water to cover the rice by 1 inch. Cover with a lid and bring to a boil, then reduce the heat and simmer for about 15 minutes until the water has been absorbed. Remove the lid, cover the pan with a clean cloth, and replace the lid. Let rest for 10 minutes.

3 Transfer the cooked rice to a large non-metal bowl. (A brown skin may have formed around the pan: simply scrape the rice away from it.) Add the vinegar, salt, and mirin, if using, and mix. For perfect sticky rice, stand it near an electric fan, stirring the rice until cooled.

4 To make the sushi rolls, toast the nori over a very low gas flame or electric hotplate for a few seconds until crisp, then put, shiny side down, on the mat or foil. Using wet fingers, put a handful of rice in the center of the nori and spread it over the top, leaving a 1 inch band uncovered nearest to you. Using the back of your finger, press a shallow groove down the middle of the rice.

5 Lay 1–2 strips of the avocado, cucumber, and bell pepper in the groove (do not overfill or you will have difficulty rolling up the sushi). Lightly sprinkle with the toasted sesame seeds.

6 Roll the mat or foil, starting from the front edge and rolling away from you, so that the rice and filling are enclosed in the nori. Dampen the edge of the nori if it doesn't stick once rolled. Remove the rolled sushi and put, join side down, in a flat container while you make the remaining rolls in the same way.

7 Using a sharp knife dipped in hot water, trim and discard the ends, then cut the roll into ½-inch thick pieces. Serve with soy sauce, pink pickled ginger, and wasabi. The sushi can be made several hours in advance, left whole, wrapped in plastic and left in a cool place until needed, but do eat on the day of making.

chocolate banana cheesecake

Chocolate and banana are natural partners in this luxuriously wicked cheesecake. Mascarpone makes the dessert lighter by reducing the cloying texture of the cream cheese.

BISCUIT BASE

8 oz. plain chocolate Milano cookies

4 tablespoons unsalted butter, melted

2 tablespoons unsweetened cocoa powder

CHEESECAKE FILLING

1 lb. cream cheese

10 oz. mascarpone cheese

2 large ripe bananas, broken into chunks

2 teaspoons pure vanilla extract

1 cup sugar

2 eggs, lightly beaten

TOPPING

4 oz. bittersweet chocolate, chopped

4 tablespoons unsalted butter, cut into cubes

1 large banana

juice of ⅛ lemon

9-inch springform cake pan, greased

SERVES 8–10

Crush the cookies in a food processor, then transfer to a bowl. Pour in the melted butter, add the cocoa, and mix well. Tip the crumbs into the prepared pan and press firmly with the back of a spoon or your fingertips. Bake in a preheated oven at 350°F for about 10 minutes. Let cool. Reduce the oven temperature to 300°F.

To make the filling, put the cheeses in a food processor and blend until smooth. Add the bananas, vanilla, and sugar and mix well. Add the eggs, a little at a time, and pulse until smooth. Alternatively, beat the ingredients, as above, in a bowl until smooth. Pour into the pan and bake for 30–40 minutes, until just set but still slightly wobbly in the middle (it will set firmer as it cools). Let cool in the pan, then chill for at least 3 hours or overnight.

To make the topping, melt the chocolate and butter in a heatproof bowl set over a saucepan of simmering water.

Unmold the cheesecake, but don't remove the bottom of the pan— the cookie base may break. Transfer to a serving plate. Top with the chocolate mixture and spread, letting it dribble over the edge. Cut the banana diagonally into long slices, toss in the lemon juice to prevent the pieces discoloring, pat dry, then arrange in a circle on top of the cheesecake. Chill until the topping is set. Serve.

sweet things

carrot and olive oil cake

Fruity olive oil makes this carrot cake like no other. Deliciously moist and lightly spiced, it couldn't be easier to make: you don't even need a mixer.

1 cup olive oil

2½ cups sugar

4 eggs, beaten

1⅔ cups all-purpose flour

2 teaspoons baking powder

2 teaspoons baking soda

2 teaspoons ground cinnamon

1 teaspoon ground cloves

1 teaspoon ground cardamom (optional)

1 teaspoon sea salt

1 cup coarsely chopped pecans or walnuts

1 lb. carrots, peeled and grated, about 3½ cups

MASCARPONE FROSTING

1¼ sticks unsalted butter, softened

2 teaspoons pure vanilla extract

1 cup mascarpone cheese or cream cheese

2 cups confectioner's sugar

9-inch springform cake pan, base-lined with wax paper, greased and lightly dusted with flour

SERVES 8–10

Put the olive oil, sugar, and eggs in a bowl and stir until well mixed. Sift the flour and other dry ingredients into a second bowl and make a well in the center. Add the egg and oil mixture and mix thoroughly until blended. Add the pecan or walnuts and carrots and mix well.

Pour into the prepared cake pan and bake in a preheated oven at 325°F for 1 hour 20 minutes, until a skewer inserted into the center comes out clean. Let cool in the pan, then run a knife around the edge of the cake to loosen and turn out.

To make the frosting, mix the butter, vanilla, and mascarpone or cream cheese in a food processor or bowl. Gradually add the confectioner's sugar and mix until smooth and creamy. Do not overmix or the frosting may curdle. Spread onto the cake and make patterns in the top.

white chocolate mousse torte

This no-bake dessert is not for the faint-hearted. You will only be able to manage a slender slice, but, believe me, it's all you need. I've had varying results with this recipe. Sometimes the texture is mousse-like, other times like truffles, but it's always divine. Serve after dinner with strong black coffee.

COOKIE BASE

about 30 amaretti cookies

1 stick unsalted butter, melted

MOUSSE

14 oz. white chocolate

2 cups heavy cream, at room temperature

¼ cup milk, at room temperature

9-inch springform cake pan, greased and lined with a collar of waxed paper

SERVES 12

Crush the amaretti cookies in a food processor until they look like fine crumbs, then transfer to a bowl and mix in the melted butter. Tip the mixture into the prepared cake pan and press firmly over the base with the back of a spoon or your fingertips.

Break the chocolate into pieces and melt in a heatproof bowl set over a saucepan of simmering water. Set aside and let cool until lukewarm.

Put the cream and milk in a bowl and, using an electric hand-held mixer, beat until the mixture leaves a ribbon-like trail on the surface when the mixer is lifted out of the bowl.

Using a large metal spoon, stir a spoonful of the whipped cream mixture into the chocolate to slacken, then immediately pour it into the remaining cream mixture. Stir vigorously until smooth and mousse-like. Don't worry if there are tiny lumps of chocolate flecked in the mixture—it will still taste delicious.

Pour into the prepared pan and swirl the top. Cover and refrigerate for at least 4 hours or overnight. When set, remove the pan, but leave the base on and peel off the paper collar. Let stand for a few minutes to soften, then cut into thin slices and serve.

raspberry roulade

Pure indulgence is a crisp meringue with a soft, marshmallow center, filled with whipped cream and topped with berries. Once mastered, you'll discover that a meringue is one of the simplest, prettiest, and most versatile of all desserts. You can use the basic recipe to make individual shells, then fill with lemon curd, cream, and seasonal fruit. Shells bake in a cool oven at 250°F for 45 minutes. Here I've used the meringue to make a feather-light roulade, which cooks in just 17 minutes. Sharp-flavored fruits, such as raspberries, balance the sweetness of the meringue, though you could use any of your favorite fruits.

MERINGUE

6 egg whites, at room temperature

a pinch of salt

2 cups superfine sugar

2 teaspoons cornstarch

1 teaspoon white wine vinegar

RASPBERRY ROSE FILLING

2 cups heavy cream

3–6 tablespoons rose water

2 cups raspberries

cookie sheet lined with wax paper
extra wax paper

SERVES 8–10

1 Put the egg whites and salt in a scrupulously clean, dry bowl and, using an electric hand-held mixer, whisk until stiff peaks form. (Take care: if there is any trace of egg yolk or moisture in the bowl the whites won't whisk properly.)

2 Sprinkle in 1 tablespoon of sugar at a time and whisk between each addition until the meringue is thick and glossy. Add the cornstarch and vinegar and whisk until mixed.

3 Transfer to the prepared cookie sheet and, using a spatula, spread the meringue into a rectangle about 12 x 16 inches. Smooth the surface. Bake in a preheated oven at 350°F for 17 minutes or until barely crisp. Let cool.

4 To turn out the meringue, cover with the extra sheet of wax paper, then quickly but carefully invert the cookie sheet onto the work surface. Lift off the sheet, then gently peel off the wax paper from the meringue.

5 To make the filling, put the cream and rose water in a bowl and whip lightly until softly peaking. Spoon onto the meringue and spread, leaving a ½-inch border clear all round. Add the raspberries.

6 Lift up the side of the wax paper nearest to you and use it to help roll up the roulade lengthwise. Peel back the paper as you go. Before you reach the end, carefully lift the roulade (still on the paper) onto a platter or board.

7 Roll the roulade off the paper so that the join is underneath, then slice into 8–10 pieces and serve.

Bright gelatins wobbling on a plate are a childhood favorite, but here are two delicious grown-up versions that you just have to try. Gelatin, though it may look and taste innocent, is not suitable for vegetarians. Luckily, there is a vegetarian alternative derived from seaweed, available from natural food stores.

gelatins and mousses

champagne gelatin

¾ **cup blueberries**

¾ **cup small seedless red grapes**

2 **cups champagne or sparkling wine**

¼ **cup superfine sugar**

3 **teaspoons vegetarian gelatin (agar agar)**

SERVES 4

Divide the blueberries and red grapes between 4 tall glasses or champagne flutes. Pour half the champagne or sparkling wine into a saucepan and add the sugar and gelatin. Heat gently, stirring until the sugar and gelatin have dissolved, then heat until almost boiling.

Slowly add the remaining champagne. Pour into the glasses and chill for 3 hours or until softly set. Serve immediately—the gelatin will soften as it nears room temperature.

thai coconut mousse

1 **cup milk**

2 **stalks lemongrass, sliced**

2 **kaffir lime leaves, coarsely chopped**

1 **inch fresh ginger, unpeeled and sliced**

1 **small red bird's eye chile, halved lengthwise**

1 **can coconut milk, about 1¾ cups**

⅔ **cup superfine sugar**

3 **teaspoons vegetarian gelatin (agar agar)**

honey-roasted peanuts, chopped, to serve

SERVES 4

Put the milk, lemongrass, lime leaves, ginger, and chile in a saucepan, bring to a boil, and simmer for 15 minutes. Let cool.

Strain the infused milk into a pitcher and add enough coconut milk to make up to 2 cups. Discard the flavorings and reserve the remaining coconut milk for another use. Return the infused milk to the pan and, using an electric hand-held mixer, beat in the sugar and gelatin until dissolved. Heat gently, beating continuously, until almost boiling, then transfer to a pitcher (for easy pouring).

Pour into 4 glass bowls. Let cool, then chill for 3 hours or until set. To serve, sprinkle with chopped peanuts.

An elegant dessert that can be made well ahead of time. For a special occasion, it's nice to stuff the pears, but, if the long list of ingredients and preparation put you off, then just omit this part. Simply serve the poached pears whole with the luscious syrup spooned over.

mulled wine pears

with spiced stuffing

4 firm, ripe pears

1 vanilla bean, split in half lengthwise

1 cup freshly squeezed orange juice

2 cups red wine

½ cup sugar

grated zest of 2 lemons

6 whole cloves

1 cinnamon stick

sour cream or crème fraîche, to serve

SPICED STUFFING

½ cup hazelnuts

1 tablespoon dark brown sugar

2 tablespoons raisins

1 teaspoon ground cinnamon

½ teaspoon ground cloves

a large pinch of freshly grated nutmeg

1½ tablespoons orange flower water

a large pinch of salt

SERVES 4

Peel the pears, leaving the stems intact. Cut a thin slice off the bottom of each one, so they stand upright, and scoop out the cores with a teaspoon. Scrape the seeds from the vanilla bean into a large saucepan, then add the bean and the orange juice, red wine, sugar, lemon zest, cloves, and cinnamon. Bring to a boil, stirring until the sugar has dissolved. Gently lower the pears on their side into the pan and simmer, turning frequently in the poaching liquid, for 30 minutes, until tender (depending on ripeness).

Using a slotted spoon, remove the pears from the poaching liquid and set aside to cool. Strain the liquid and return to the pan. Heat until reduced and syrupy. Let cool.

To make the stuffing, roast the hazelnuts in a preheated oven at 400°F for 5 minutes, until lightly golden. Let cool. Put in a food processor, pulse until ground, then add the remaining ingredients and pulse until mixed. Spoon the mixture into the hollowed-out poached pears and spread a thin layer on the bottom of each one (this will help the pears stand upright when you put them on the plates). Serve with the syrup poured over and a dollop of sour cream or crème fraîche.

2 sticks unsalted butter

1 cup raw sugar

⅔ cup honey

4 cups rolled oats

⅓ cup chopped nuts, dried fruits, or glacé ginger, or unsweetened desiccated coconut (optional)

a 8 x 12 inch shallow cake pan, greased

MAKES 12

Put the butter, sugar, and honey in a saucepan and heat, stirring occasionally, until the butter has melted and the sugar has dissolved. Add the oats and nuts, dried fruit, glacé ginger, or coconut, if using, and mix well.

Transfer the oat mixture to the prepared cake pan and spread to about 1 inch thick. Smooth the surface with the back of a spoon. Bake in a preheated oven at 350°F for 15–20 minutes, until lightly golden around the edges, but still slightly soft in the middle.

Let cool in the pan, then turn out and cut into squares.

honey oat bars

These wonderful chewy oat bars are practically effortless to make. You don't have to be an expert baker to have a go. Oat bars are perfect teatime treats or mid-morning snacks. They also travel well—wrap for a picnic or packed lunch.

chocolate chunk nut cookies

Simple to make, absolutely divine taste, crisp on the outside, soft and gooey in the middle—what more could you ask for? Vary the nuts to suit yourself: I'm fond of pecans, macadamias, and pine nuts, but you can use walnuts or hazelnuts. Keep the chocolate and nuts chunky for maximum impact.

1 cup all-purpose flour

1/2 teaspoon baking powder

1/2 teaspoon salt

1 1/4 sticks unsalted butter, softened

1/2 cup dark brown sugar

1 teaspoon pure vanilla extract

1 egg

8 oz. bittersweet chocolate, coarsely chopped

1/3 cup coarsely chopped nuts, such as pecans or hazelnuts

a large baking sheet, lined with wax paper

MAKES 12–14

Put all the ingredients, except the chocolate and nuts, in a food processor and blend until mixed. Stir in the chocolate and nuts. Alternatively, sift the flour, baking powder and salt into a bowl. Put the butter, sugar, and vanilla in another bowl and beat with a wooden spoon or electric mixer, until light and fluffy. Gradually beat in the egg. Fold in the flour mixture. Mix in the chocolate and nuts.

Scrape the cookie dough onto a large square of plastic wrap and roll into a 12-inch long sausage shape. Twist the ends to seal and chill for at least 30 minutes or until firm.

When ready to bake, unwrap the dough and cut into 1-inch thick slices. Put 1 inch apart on the prepared baking sheet (in batches, if necessary) and bake in a preheated oven at 375°F for 15–20 minutes, until just golden. Transfer to a wire rack to cool.

menu ideas

JAPANESE LUNCH

Vegetarian sushi roll

Japanese omelet

Grilled asparagus and leaf salad
with sesame-soy dressing

THAI SUPPER

Thai coleslaw

Pad Thai noodles

Thai coconut mousses

LIGHT MIDDLE EASTERN LUNCH

Babaganouj with warm flatbread

Warm chickpea salad with
spiced mushrooms

A FEAST FOR THE EYES

*(a particularly beautiful but not too
complicated meal)*

Pumpkin and tofu laksa

Raspberry roulade

SUMMER SALAD FEAST

Saffron potato salad

Tuscan panzanella

Minted grilled zucchini

Green salad with blue cheese
dressing I

MEXICAN INDIAN SUMMER SUPPER

Mexican gazpacho

Haloumi fajitas

Chocolate banana cheesecake

BARBECUE I

Parmesan patties

Feta-stuffed peppers

Thai-glazed vegetable skewers

Caesar salad

BARBECUE II

Turkish stuffed eggplant

Stuffed flat mushrooms with
mozzarella and truffle oil

Thai-glazed vegetable skewers

Grilled asparagus and leaf salad
with sesame-soy dressing

MEXICAN ALL-YEAR SUPPER OR LUNCH

Quesadillas

Tamales

Chocolate banana cheesecake

WARMING WINTER DINNER

Shiitake and field mushroom soup
with Madeira and thyme

Braised Belgian endive and beans
with smoked cheese mash

Raspberry roulade

DEEP-HEAT WINTER LUNCH

Lemon-potato latkes with gingered
avocado crème

Charred eggplant and coconut curry

Carrot and olive oil cake

SIMPLE WINTER LUNCH

Caramelized onion and Gruyère
focaccia

Lentil, coconut, and wilted spinach
soup

**ITALIAN DINNER WITH POLENTA
IN TWO GUISES**

Stuffed polenta mushrooms

Piedmontese peppers with
gorgonzola polenta

VEGETARIAN CHRISTMAS I

Celeriac, saffron, and orange soup

Chestnut, spinach, and mushroom
phyllo torte

Lemon-roasted new potatoes

Greens with pine nuts and
redcurrants (see Chile greens with
crispy garlic)

Mulled wine pears with spiced
stuffing

VEGETARIAN CHRISTMAS II

Bruschetta with wild mushrooms
and apples in a creamy Madeira
sauce

Torta di risotto with three cheeses

Chile greens with crispy garlic

Roasted sweet potatoes with
shallots, garlic, and chiles

White chocolate mousse torte

CHRISTMAS DRINKS PARTY

Mushroom and onion marmalade
tartlets

Spinach and water chestnut
wontons

Lemon potato latkes with gingered
avocado crème

Spiced roasted nuts

Stuffed polenta mushrooms

SUMMER DRINKS PARTY

Vegetarian sushi roll

Mozzarella and cherry tomato
skewers

Feta and cumin phyllo parcels

Crudités with sesame yogurt dip

Topped Bruschetta with slow-
roasted tomatoes

A LUNCH OF SMALL COURSES

Babaganouj and sesame yogurt dip
with warm flatbread

Topped bruschetta with wild
mushrooms

Piedmontese peppers

Champagne gelatins

FUSS-FREE AUTUMN DINNER

Shiitake and field mushroom soup
with Madeira and thyme

Vegetarian sausages and mashed
potatoes with thyme and
mushroom gravy

Provençal roasted vegetables

Raspberry roulade

FULL-ON BRUNCH BUFFET FOR 14

Cottage cheese pancakes with
berries, jelly, and crème fraîche

Japanese omelet with grilled
tomatoes and avocado

Breakfast burritos

Corn muffins

Caesar salad

Honey oat bars

Chocolate chunk nut cookies

index

WEIGHTS AND MEASURES: CONVERSION CHARTS

Weights and measures have been rounded up or down
slightly to make measuring easier.

VOLUME EQUIVALENTS

American	Metric	Imperial
1 teaspoon	5 ml	
1 tablespoon	15 ml	
¼ cup	60 ml	2 fl.oz.
⅓ cup	75 ml	2½ fl.oz.
½ cup	125 ml	4 fl.oz.
⅔ cup	150 ml	5 fl.oz. (¼ pint)
¾ cup	175 ml	6 fl.oz.
1 cup	250 ml	8 fl.oz.

WEIGHT EQUIVALENTS

Imperial	Metric
1 oz.	25 g
2 oz.	50 g
3 oz.	75 g
4 oz.	125 g
5 oz.	150 g
6 oz.	175 g
7 oz.	200 g
8 oz. (½ lb.)	250 g
9 oz.	275 g
10 oz.	300 g
11 oz.	325 g
12 oz.	375 g
13 oz.	400 g
14 oz.	425 g
15 oz.	475 g
16 oz. (1 lb.)	500 g
2 1b.	1 kg

MEASUREMENTS

inches	cm
¼ inch	5 mm
½ inch	1 cm
¾ inch	1.5 cm
1 inch	2.5 cm
2 inches	5 cm
3 inches	7 cm
4 inches	10 cm
5 inches	12 cm
6 inches	15 cm
7 inches	18 cm
8 inches	20 cm
9 inches	23 cm
10 inches	25 cm
11 inches	28 cm
12 inches	30 cm

OVEN TEMPERATURES

110°C	(225°F)	Gas ¼
120°C	(250°F)	Gas ½
140°C	(275°F)	Gas 1
150°C	(300°F)	Gas 2
160°C	(325°F)	Gas 3
180°C	(350°F)	Gas 4
190°C	(375°F)	Gas 5
200°C	(400°F)	Gas 6
220°C	(425°F)	Gas 7
230°C	(450°F)	Gas 8
240°C	(475°F)	Gas 9

FOOD & WINE

quick from scratch
chicken cookbook

FOOD & WINE

quick from scratch
chicken cookbook

FOOD & WINE
BOOKS

FOOD & WINE

Editor Judith Hill
Assistant Editors Susan Lantzius and Laura Byrne Russell
Managing Editor Terri Mauro
Copy Editor Barbara A. Mateer
Wine Editor Richard Marmet
Art Director Nina Scerbo
Art Assistant Leslie Andersen
Photographer Melanie Acevedo
Food Stylist Roscoe Betsill
Prop Stylist Denise Canter

V.P., Books and Products/Publisher Marshall Corey
Director, Book Programs Bruce Spanier
Senior Marketing Manager, Branded Books Eric Lucie
Assistant Marketing Manager Lizabeth Clark
Director of Fulfillment & Premium Value Phil Black
**Manager of Customer Experience &
   Product Development** Charles Graver
Director of Finance Thomas Noonan
Associate Business Manager Desiree Bernardez

AMERICAN EXPRESS PUBLISHING CORPORATION

President/C.E.O. Ed Kelly
S.V.P./Chief Marketing Officer Mark V. Stanich
**C.F.O./S.V.P./Corporate Development &
   Operations** Paul B. Francis
V.P./General Managers Frank Bland, Keith Strohmeier

Time Inc.
HOME ENTERTAINMENT

Publisher Richard Fraiman
General Manager Steven Sandonato
Executive Director, Marketing Services Carol Pittard
Director, Retail & Special Sales Tom Mifsud
Director, New Product Development Peter Harper
Director of Trade Marketing Sydney Webber
Assistant Director, Bookazine Marketing Laura Adam
Assistant Director, Brand Marketing Joy Butts
Associate Counsel Helen Wan
Associate Manager, Product Marketing Nina Fleishman
Design & Prepress Manager Anne-Michelle Gallero
Book Production Manager Susan Chodakiewicz

Special thanks
Glenn Buonocore, Lauren Hall, Margaret Hess,
Jennifer Jacobs, Suzanne Janso, Brynn Joyce,
Robert Marasco, Amy Migliaccio, Brooke Reger,
Ilene Schreider, Adriana Tierno, Alex Voznesenskiy

DOWNTOWN BOOKWORKS INC.

President Julie Merberg
Senior Vice President Patty Brown
Copy Editor Sara Newberry
Indexer Stephen Callahan
Designer Anne-Michelle Gallero

Special thanks Sarah Parvis, Pam Abrams

table of contents

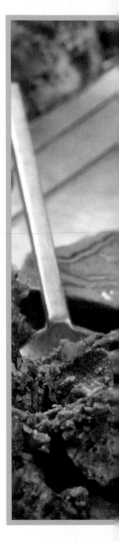

before you begin

You'll find test-kitchen tips and ideas for ingredient substitutions presented with the individual recipes throughout the book. In this opening section, we've gathered information and tips that apply to all, or at least a substantial number, of the recipes. These are the facts and opinions that we'd like you to know before you use, and to keep in mind while you use, the recipes. We hope you'll read these pages prior to cooking from the book for the first time—and have kept the section short so that you can do so with ease. The culinary information here will help make your cooking quicker, simpler, and even tastier.

substituting parts—or birds

If you like white meat and the recipe calls for dark (or vice versa), or if you want to interchange Cornish hens and chicken, by all means do so. Simply increase or decrease cooking time according to the times given in our chart. These guidelines are based on chickens that weigh 3 to 3½ pounds and Cornish hens of about 1¼ pounds. The cooking times are necessarily approximate, but they'll get you close to the mark.

INSTEAD OF	USE	COOKING METHOD	COOKING TIME
Legs			
4 whole bone-in legs	4 bone-in individual breasts	Roast, sauté, grill	5 min. less
		Simmer	10 min. less
8 bone-in thighs or drumsticks	4 bone-in individual breasts	Roast, sauté, grill	4 min. less
		Simmer	8 min. less
4 boneless, skinless thighs	4 boneless, skinless breasts	Sauté, grill	4 min. less
		Simmer	5 min. less
Cut-up boneless, skinless thighs	Cut-up boneless, skinless breasts	All methods	1 to 2 min. less
Breasts			
4 bone-in individual breasts	4 whole bone-in legs	Roast, sauté, grill	5 min. more
		Simmer	10 min. more
4 bone-in individual breasts	8 bone-in thighs or drumsticks	Roast, sauté, grill	4 min. more
		Simmer	8 min. more
4 boneless, skinless breasts	4 boneless, skinless thighs	Sauté, grill	4 min. more
		Simmer	5 min. more
Cut-up boneless, skinless breasts	Cut-up boneless, skinless thighs	All methods	1 to 2 min. more

INSTEAD OF	USE	COOKING METHOD	COOKING TIME
Wings			
2 pounds wings	4 bone-in individual breasts	Roast, sauté, grill	2 to 5 min. more
2 pounds wings	8 thighs or drumsticks	Roast, sauté, grill	5 to 10 min. more
Whole or Half Chicken			
1 chicken	2 Cornish hens	Roast	15 min. less
2 chicken halves	4 Cornish-hen halves	Grill	10 min. less
Cornish Hens			
2 Cornish hens	1 chicken	Roast	15 min. more
4 Cornish-hen halves	2 chicken halves	Grill	10 min. more
Turkey			
Turkey cutlets	Chicken cutlets	Sauté, grill	Same
Turkey sausage	Chicken sausage	Sauté, grill	Same
Ground turkey	Ground chicken	Sauté, grill	Same

essential
ingredient information

Broth, Chicken

We tested all of the recipes in this book using canned low-sodium chicken broth. You can almost always substitute regular for low-sodium broth; just cut back on the salt in the recipe. And if you keep homemade stock in your freezer, by all means feel free to use it. We aren't suggesting that it won't work as well, only that we know the dishes taste delicious even when made with canned broth.

Butter

Our recipes don't specify whether to use salted or unsalted butter. We generally use unsalted, but in these savory dishes, it really won't make a big difference which type you use.

Garlic

The size of garlic cloves varies tremendously. When we call for one minced or chopped clove, we expect you to get about three-quarters of a teaspoon.

Milk, Coconut

Coconut milk is the traditional liquid used in many Thai and Indian curries. Make sure you buy unsweetened canned coconut milk, not cream of coconut, which is used primarily for piña coladas. Heavy cream can be substituted in many recipes.

Mustard

When we call for mustard, we mean Dijon or grainy. We never, ever mean yellow ballpark mustard.

Nuts

Our quick pantry wouldn't be complete without several kinds of nuts. Keep in mind that nuts have a high percentage of oil and can turn rancid quickly. We store ours in the freezer to keep them fresh.

Oil

Cooking oil in these recipes refers to readily available, reasonably priced nut, seed, or vegetable oil with a high smoking point, such as peanut, sunflower, canola, safflower, or corn oil. These can be heated to about 400° before they begin to smoke, break down, and develop an unpleasant flavor.

Olives

If your store doesn't sell olives from big, open barrels, opt for the kind in jars. The canned version gives you only the slightest hint of what a real olive might taste like.

Parsley

Many of our recipes call for chopped fresh parsley. The flat-leaf variety has a stronger flavor than the curly, and we use it most of the time, but unless the type is specified, you can use either.

Pepper

• There's nothing like fresh-ground pepper. If you've been using preground, buy a pepper mill, fill it, and give it a grind. You'll never look back.
• To measure your just-ground pepper more easily, become familiar with your own mill; each produces a different amount per turn. You'll probably find that ten to fifteen grinds produces one-quarter teaspoon of pepper, and then you can count on that forever after.

Sausages, Chicken and Turkey

While testing recipes for this book, we found tremendous differences in the quality and flavor of chicken and turkey sausages. Try various kinds to find your favorite.

Tomatoes, Canned

In some recipes, we call for "crushed tomatoes in thick puree." Depending on the brand, this mix of crushed tomatoes and tomato puree may be labeled crushed tomatoes with puree, with added puree, in tomato puree, thick style, or in thick puree. You can use any of these.

Wine, Dry White

Leftover wine is ideal for cooking. It seems a shame to open a fresh bottle for just a few spoonfuls. Another solution is to keep dry vermouth on hand. You can use whatever quantity is needed; the rest will keep indefinitely.

Zest

Citrus zest—the colored part of the peel, without any of the white pith—adds tremendous flavor to many a dish. Remove the zest from the fruit using either a grater or a zester. A zester is a small, inexpensive, and extremely handy tool with little holes that remove just the zest in fine ribbons. A zester is quick, easy to clean, and never scrapes your knuckles.

faster, better, easier
test-kitchen tips

Defrosting chicken

We prefer to use fresh chicken, which always has juicier meat than frozen, but everybody freezes chicken at some time or another. When you do, remember that the method of defrosting affects the texture. We tested common methods on frozen chicken quarters.

• MICROWAVE: *Quickest*. Good quality. We microwaved quartered chickens on the defrost setting for 22 minutes. When roasted, the meat wasn't quite as juicy as fresh but was still moist. Just be sure to keep an eye on the chicken while it's defrosting; don't let it cook.

• REFRIGERATOR: *Slowest*. Best quality. Defrosting chicken in the refrigerator results in juicy meat, most like that of fresh. The only problem is that you need to think ahead; quartered chickens take a good 24 hours to defrost.

• WARM RUNNING WATER: *Least successful*. We ran warm water over the frozen chicken quarters for 45 minutes to defrost. When cooked, the chicken was dry and stringy. We don't recommend this method.

Measuring spoons

We've found that measuring spoons with well rounded bottoms are the most accurate. Avoid the ones that are extremely shallow; they can be off by almost 50 percent.

Don't crowd chicken when browning

To brown chicken, use a pan large enough to hold all the pieces with at least half an inch between them. We recommend a 10-inch frying pan or pot. When chicken is crowded, the heat drops, and the pieces stew rather than brown. If your pan isn't wide enough, brown the chicken in two batches.

Quick-kitchen method for carving chicken

To cut up a roast chicken quickly, use primarily your hands and a pair of kitchen scissors. We like Joyce Chen® scissors, which are ideally engineered with large, round handles enclosed in plastic and short, sharp blades.

- BREASTS: Start with a knife. Cut along one side of the breast bone and then slide the knife blade along the bones, cutting the meat off the bone as you go. After that use scissors. Break the wing joint attached to the bird and cut through it so that the wing stays attached to the breast meat. Cut the breast in half crosswise. Do the same with the other breast.
- LEGS: Bend each leg back exposing the joint. Break the joint and then cut through it and along the backbone to release the leg from the carcass. Cut it into drumstick and thigh.

Avoid cooking poultry too long

Perfectly cooked poultry is juicy, tender, and tempting. Unfortunately, once overcooked, it's tough and dry. The breast is particularly susceptible to overcooking, not to mention diced chicken or turkey.

- CHICKEN BREASTS: Nothing beats boneless, skinless breasts for fast cooking. So we have loads of recipes for them in this book, most of which require only 10 minutes cooking time. Don't allow the breasts to overcook. Without the protection of the bone, they quickly become dry and disappointing.
- TURKEY CUTLETS: Cut from the breast, these are usually about one quarter-inch thick. Cooking takes 1 to 2 minutes per side at the most (rarely longer than 3 minutes total). If you cook them longer, they will be dry. We know it's hard to make yourself take a cutlet out of the pan almost as soon as you put it in, but trust us, you'll be glad you did.
- DICED POULTRY: Small pieces of chicken or turkey can turn into hard little balls in a flash. Simmer or poach diced poultry at a low temperature. Never allow the liquid to boil, which makes the meat fibrous and dry.

Oven accuracy

It's not unusual for the actual temperature in your oven to vary wildly from the setting. To save your roasted and baked chickens from disaster, invest in an oven thermometer, take your oven's temperature occasionally, and adjust the setting accordingly.

Yellow-skinned chicken

Some varieties of supermarket chicken have a yellow tint to their skin, which is a result of the birds' feed. We find the color doesn't affect flavor, but the golden-hued poultry does seem to brown better than its fair-skinned counterpart.

Test for doneness

We think the classic method is the best way to check for doneness: Stick a small, sharp knife into the inside of the thigh. If the juices run clear, the chicken is done. If the juices are pink, continue cooking. This test applies to whole chickens, halves, and parts.

Golden-brown skin

If you're nearing the end of the roasting time and your chicken isn't quite as brown as you'd like, slide it under the broiler for the last few minutes of cooking. The skin should crisp right up.

The fastest way to peel garlic

Use a large knife to peel a garlic clove. Put the flat side of the blade over the garlic and smack the blade with your fist or the heel of your hand. The clove will crack, and the skin will loosen and come off easily.

Chicken Noodle Soup with
Parsnips & Dill on page 40.

2

soups, stews, curries, & other braised dishes

kale & potato soup with turkey sausage

Traditional Portuguese kale and potato soup inspired this delicious country-style dish. It's especially welcome in the winter months when kale is at its peak.

PREP TIME 6 MINUTES   **COOK TIME** 30 MINUTES

SERVES 4

1	tablespoon cooking oil
1	pound turkey or chicken sausage
1	onion, chopped
4	cloves garlic, cut into thin slices
1	quart water
2	cups canned low-sodium chicken broth or homemade stock
1½	teaspoons salt
1½	pounds boiling potatoes, peeled and cut into ¼-inch pieces
	Pinch dried red-pepper flakes
1	pound kale, stems removed, leaves shredded
¼	teaspoon fresh-ground black pepper

1. In a large pot, heat the oil over moderately low heat. Add the sausage and cook, turning, until browned, about 10 minutes. Remove the sausage from the pot and, when it is cool enough to handle, cut it into slices. Pour off all but 1 tablespoon fat from the pan.

2. Add the onion and cook, stirring occasionally, until it is translucent, about 5 minutes. Add the garlic to the pan and cook, stirring, for 1 minute longer.

3. Add the water, broth, and salt and bring the soup to a boil. Add the sausage, potatoes, and red-pepper flakes and bring back to a simmer. Cook, partially covered, for 2 minutes. Add the kale and bring the soup back to a simmer. Cook, partially covered, until the potatoes and kale are tender, about 6 minutes longer. Add the black pepper.

MENU SUGGESTIONS

An interesting bread completes this meal with aplomb. Try corn bread or tomato-topped Italian focaccia. A good crusty loaf of white bread will do fine, too.

wine recommendation

An aromatic, acidic white wine such as a sauvignon blanc is always a great choice for leafy greens. But the heartiness of this country soup can also work well with a full-bodied Portuguese red wine such as a Dão.

spicy chicken chili

This spicy stew is a surefire way to please everyone at the table. Leftover turkey or chicken can be substituted for the chicken thighs.

PREP TIME 10 MINUTES   COOK TIME 40 MINUTES
SERVES 4

2	tablespoons cooking oil
1	onion, chopped
2	cloves garlic, minced
1	pound boneless skinless chicken thighs (about 4), cut into thin strips
4	teaspoons chili powder
1	tablespoon ground cumin
2	teaspoons dried oregano
1	teaspoon salt
2	jalapeño peppers, seeds and ribs removed, chopped
1½	cups canned crushed tomatoes with their juice
2½	cups canned low-sodium chicken broth or homemade stock
1⅔	cups drained and rinsed pinto beans from one 15-ounce can)
1⅔	cups drained and rinsed black beans (from one 15-ounce can)
½	teaspoon fresh-ground black pepper
⅓	cup chopped cilantro (optional)

1. In a large saucepan, heat the oil over moderately low heat. Add the onion and garlic; cook until they start to soften, about 3 minutes.

2. Increase the heat to moderate and stir in the chicken strips. Cook until they are no longer pink, about 2 minutes. Stir in the chili powder, cumin, oregano, and salt. Add the jalapeños, the tomatoes with their juice, and the broth. Bring to a boil, reduce the heat, cover, and simmer for 15 minutes.

3. Uncover the saucepan and stir in the beans and black pepper. Simmer until the chili is thickened, about 15 minutes longer. Serve topped with the cilantro.

MENU SUGGESTIONS
Wedges of corn bread are always a good complement to chili. Or serve the chili over macaroni or rice.

wine recommendation

A red wine with plenty of acidity is best suited to the spice and heat here. Look for a sangiovese from California or a dolcetto from the Piedmont region of Italy.

groundnut stew

Peanut butter and okra flavor and thicken this tasty African stew. You can substitute green beans for the okra, if you like; the consistency of the sauce won't be quite the same, but it will still be thick enough to cling to the chicken.

PREP TIME 5 MINUTES   **COOK TIME** 35 MINUTES
SERVES 4

2	tablespoons cooking oil, more if needed
1	chicken (3 to 3½ pounds), cut into 8 pieces
1¾	teaspoons salt
½	teaspoon fresh-ground black pepper
1	onion, chopped
2	tablespoons tomato paste
1	cup canned crushed tomatoes, drained
¼	teaspoon cayenne
2¾	cups water
½	cup creamy peanut butter
1	10-ounce package frozen sliced okra

1. In a large pot, heat the oil over moderately high heat. Season the chicken pieces with ¼ teaspoon each of the salt and black pepper. Cook until browned, turning, about 8 minutes in all. Remove. Pour off all but 1 tablespoon fat from the pot.

2. Reduce the heat to moderately low. Add the onion to the pot and cook, stirring occasionally, until starting to soften, about 3 minutes. Stir in the tomato paste and then the tomatoes and cayenne. Return the chicken legs and thighs to the pot and stir in 2 cups of the water. Bring to a simmer and cook, partially covered, for 10 minutes.

3. Whisk together the peanut butter and the remaining ¾ cup water until smooth. Add this mixture to the stew along with the chicken breasts and wings, the okra and the remaining 1½ teaspoons of salt and ¼ teaspoon of black pepper. Cook, partially covered, until the okra is just done, about 10 minutes.

MENU SUGGESTIONS
Serve the stew with rice or egg noodles to capture every drop of the distinctive sauce.

wine recommendation
A simple, fruity red wine such as a Beaujolais (or, if it's December through March, a Beaujolais Nouveau) will make a lively companion to the peanut butter in this stew.

chicken stew with cider & parsnips

Carrots, parsnips, and chicken simmer in a sauce of apple cider and chicken broth, making a delicious and homey stew—perfect for a chilly fall evening.

PREP TIME 5 MINUTES   **COOK TIME** 40 MINUTES
SERVES 4

2	tablespoons cooking oil
4	chicken thighs
4	chicken drumsticks
¾	teaspoon salt
¼	teaspoon fresh-ground black pepper
1	tablespoon flour
1	cup apple cider
1½	cups canned low-sodium chicken broth or homemade stock
1	onion, cut into thin slices
1	pound parsnips, cut into 1-inch pieces
2	carrots, cut into 1-inch pieces
½	teaspoon dried thyme

1. Heat the oven to 400°. In a large pot or Dutch oven, heat the oil over moderately high heat. Season the chicken thighs and drumsticks with ¼ teaspoon of the salt and the pepper.

Cook the chicken until browned, turning, about 8 minutes in all. Remove. Pour off all but 1 tablespoon of the fat from the pot.

2. Reduce the heat to moderate and stir in the flour. Whisk in the cider and the broth and bring to a simmer, scraping the bottom of the pot to dislodge any brown bits. Add the onion, parsnips, carrots, thyme, and the remaining ½ teaspoon of salt. Simmer, partially covered, for 10 minutes.

3. Return the chicken to the pot. Bring the stew back to a simmer, cover, and put in the preheated oven until the chicken is done and the vegetables are tender, about 15 minutes.

MENU SUGGESTIONS

Simple boiled potatoes, egg noodles, or rice would be perfect for catching the stew's extra sauce.

wine recommendation

A "comfort" wine will make this dish even more satisfying. A rustic red from the south of France, such as a Cahors or Minervois, is a good possibility.

indian-spiced chicken & spinach

The flavor of this dish is rich, fragrant, and mellow—not hot. You can make the sauce ahead of time and simmer the chicken in it just before serving.

PREP TIME 8 MINUTES   **COOK TIME** 25 MINUTES

SERVES 4

2	tablespoons cooking oil
1	onion, chopped
3	cloves garlic, chopped
1	tablespoon chopped fresh ginger
1	tablespoon ground cumin
1	tablespoon ground coriander
½	teaspoon turmeric
½	teaspoon paprika
1½	teaspoons salt
2	jalapeño peppers, seeds and ribs removed, minced
½	cup canned crushed tomatoes, drained
½	cup heavy cream
1	cinnamon stick
1½	cups water
2	10-ounce packages frozen chopped spinach, thawed
4	boneless, skinless chicken breasts (about 1⅓ pounds in all), cut into 3 pieces each

1. In a large frying pan, heat the oil over moderately low heat. Add the onion and cook until starting to soften, about 3 minutes. Add the garlic and ginger and cook, stirring occasionally, for 2 minutes longer. Stir in the cumin, coriander, turmeric, paprika, and 1 teaspoon of the salt. Cook until the spices are fragrant, about 1 minute, and then stir in the jalapeños and tomatoes. Add the cream, cinnamon stick, and water. Squeeze the spinach to remove excess liquid and add the spinach to the pan. Bring to a simmer. Cover the pan, reduce the heat, and simmer for 5 minutes.

2. Stir in the chicken and the remaining ½ teaspoon salt, cover, and simmer the stew until just done, about 10 minutes. Remove the cinnamon stick before serving.

MENU SUGGESTIONS

Indian basmati rice would be an ideal accompaniment here, but plain white rice will work well, too.

wine recommendation

An off-dry chenin blanc from California or a chenin-blanc–based French Vouvray (look for a demi-sec) will be lovely with the aromatic cream sauce. The acidity of these wines and their melon and apricot notes are perfect foils for the exotic stew.

massaman curry

So many curries are made throughout the world that it's hard to pick favorites. But this dish, based on a Thai and Muslim combination including potatoes, peanuts, and five-spice powder, must be one of the best.

PREP TIME 10 MINUTES   **COOK TIME** 30 MINUTES
SERVES 4

1	tablespoon cooking oil
1	onion, chopped
2	cloves garlic, minced
1	teaspoon chopped fresh ginger
1	teaspoon Chinese five-spice powder
1	teaspoon ground cumin
¼	teaspoon cayenne
¼	teaspoon turmeric
1	teaspoon salt
1	cup canned low-sodium chicken broth or homemade stock
½	cup canned unsweetened coconut milk or heavy cream
½	pound boiling potatoes (about 2), peeled and cut into ½-inch pieces
1 ⅓	pounds boneless, skinless chicken breasts (about 4), cut into ½-inch pieces
½	cup chopped peanuts
½	pound plum tomatoes (about 4), cut into wedges
3	tablespoons chopped cilantro

1. In a large saucepan, heat the oil over moderately low heat. Add the onion and cook, stirring occasionally, until it is translucent, about 5 minutes. Add the garlic, ginger, five-spice powder, cumin, cayenne, turmeric, and ½ teaspoon of the salt. Stir until fragrant, about 1 minute. Whisk in the broth and then the coconut milk; bring to a simmer. Stir in the potatoes, cover, and cook over low heat until they are almost tender, about 12 minutes.

2. Add the chicken to the sauce, cover, and simmer for 5 minutes. Stir in the peanuts, tomatoes, cilantro, and the remaining ½ teaspoon salt. Turn the heat off, cover, and let steam until the chicken is just done, about 2 minutes longer.

MENU SUGGESTIONS
For this curry, steamed white rice is the only accompaniment you need.

wine recommendation

For this bold curry, bursting with heat, spice, and sweetness, a fresh, aromatic white that won't get pushed around—a chenin blanc from the Loire Valley in France or from California, for example, or a sauvignon blanc from New Zealand—is a good match.

spiced chicken legs with apricots & raisins

Fruity and peppery, this exotic dish will perk up your midweek menu. Yet it's no more trouble than the simplest chicken recipe in your repertoire.

PREP TIME 6 MINUTES   **COOK TIME** 35 MINUTES

SERVES 4

2	tablespoons cooking oil
4	chicken thighs
4	chicken drumsticks
1¾	teaspoons salt
½	teaspoon fresh-ground black pepper
1	onion, chopped
3	cloves garlic, chopped
1¼	cups canned low-sodium chicken broth or homemade stock
¼	teaspoon allspice
¼	teaspoon red-pepper flakes
⅔	cup dried apricots, quartered
¼	cup dark or golden raisins
¼	cup chopped fresh parsley

1. In a large, deep frying pan, heat the oil over moderately high heat. Season the chicken thighs and drumsticks with ¼ teaspoon each of the salt and pepper. Cook the chicken until browned, turning, about 8 minutes in all. Remove. Pour off all but 1 tablespoon of the fat from the pan.

2. Reduce the heat to moderately low. Add the onion and garlic to the pan; cook, stirring occasionally, until the onion starts to soften, about 3 minutes. Add the broth, the remaining 1½ teaspoons salt and ¼ teaspoon black pepper, the allspice, and the red-pepper flakes. Add the chicken, apricots, and raisins. Bring to a simmer, reduce the heat, and simmer the chicken, partially covered, until just done, about 20 minutes. Serve topped with the parsley.

MENU SUGGESTIONS

Couscous is a natural with this Moroccan-inspired dish.

wine recommendation

The sweetness here will be nicely mirrored by an off-dry, aromatic white wine, such as a chenin blanc, riesling, or gewürztraminer from California.

rustic garlic chicken

Yes, three heads of garlic. You don't have to peel the cloves first. They soften during cooking and take on a subtle sweetness. Each person squeezes the garlic out of its skin onto the plate to eat with the chicken.

PREP TIME 5 MINUTES　　**COOK TIME** 30 MINUTES

SERVES 4

2	tablespoons cooking oil
1.	chicken (about 3 to 3 ½ pounds), cut into 8 pieces
1	teaspoon salt
¼	teaspoon fresh-ground black pepper
3	heads garlic, cloves separated
2	tablespoons flour
1	cup dry white wine
1	cup canned low-sodium chicken broth or homemade stock
2	tablespoons butter
2	tablespoons chopped fresh parsley

1. Heat the oven to 400°. In a Dutch oven, heat the oil over moderately high heat. Sprinkle the chicken with ½ teaspoon of the salt and the pepper. Cook the chicken until well browned, turning, about 8 minutes in all, and remove from the pot. Reduce the heat to moderate, add the garlic, and sauté until it is starting to brown, about 3 minutes. Sprinkle the flour over the garlic and stir until combined. Return the chicken to the pot, cover, and bake for 15 minutes.

2. Remove the pot from the oven and put it on a burner. Remove the chicken pieces from the pot. Over moderately high heat, whisk in the wine and simmer for 1 minute. Whisk in the broth and the remaining ½ teaspoon salt and simmer until starting to thicken, about 3 minutes. Turn the heat off, whisk in the butter, and pour the sauce over the chicken. Sprinkle with the parsley.

MENU SUGGESTIONS

There's plenty of luscious, garlicky sauce here. Take advantage of it with mashed potatoes, egg noodles, or rice.

wine recommendation

This simple Gallic dish will work well with a rustic red wine from the south of France. Look for lesser-known, good-value bottles from Corbières or Minervois, or a more serious, tannic wine from Cahors.

chicken goulash

Fragrant with paprika and brimming with flavor, this Hungarian classic continues to please. Our quick version loses none of the original appeal.

PREP TIME 8 MINUTES   COOK TIME 35 MINUTES
SERVES 4

1   tablespoon cooking oil
8   chicken thighs
1½   teaspoons salt
1   onion, chopped
2   carrots, cut into ¼-inch slices
2   ribs celery, cut into ¼-inch slices
2   cloves garlic, minced
2   tablespoons paprika
1   tablespoon flour
⅛   teaspoon cayenne
1½   cups canned low-sodium chicken broth
     or homemade stock
1½   cups canned crushed tomatoes in thick puree
¼   teaspoon dried thyme
1   bay leaf
2   tablespoons chopped fresh parsley
¼   teaspoon fresh-ground black pepper

1. In a large, heavy pot, heat the oil over moderately high heat. Season the chicken with ¼ teaspoon of the salt and add it to the pan. Cook the chicken until browned, turning, about 8 minutes in all. Remove. Pour off all but 1 tablespoon fat from the pan.

2. Add the onion, carrots, celery, and garlic to the pan. Reduce the heat to moderate and cook, stirring occasionally, until the onion is translucent, about 5 minutes.

3. Reduce the heat to moderately low and add the paprika, flour, and cayenne to the pan. Cook, stirring, for 30 seconds. Stir in the broth, tomatoes, the remaining 1¼ teaspoons salt, the thyme, and the bay leaf. Add the chicken and bring to a simmer. Reduce the heat and simmer, partially covered, until the chicken is done, about 20 minutes. Remove the bay leaf and add the parsley and black pepper.

MENU SUGGESTIONS
Serve the goulash with spaetzle, buttered noodles, or boiled or mashed potatoes.

wine recommendation
With this dish, it's natural to experiment with one of the increasing number of reds imported from Hungary. Try Egri Bikavér or a varietal such as a merlot or a cabernet sauvignon.

chicken & cavatelli

So comforting and yummy, this dish reminds us of Grandma's chicken and dumplings. In fact, you can substitute frozen dumplings for the cavatelli.

PREP TIME 6 MINUTES   COOK TIME 35 MINUTES
SERVES 4

5   cups canned low-sodium chicken broth
     or homemade stock
1   bay leaf
1   onion, cut into thin slices
2   ribs celery, cut into ½-inch pieces
3   carrots, cut into ½-inch pieces
1   teaspoon dried sage
1½   teaspoons salt
¼   teaspoon fresh-ground black pepper
4   bone-in chicken breasts (about 2¼ pounds in all)
¾   pound frozen cavatelli, egg noodles, or dumplings
2   tablespoons butter, softened
2   tablespoons flour

1. In a large pot, bring the broth, bay leaf, onion, celery, and carrots to a simmer. Simmer for 5 minutes. Add the sage, salt, pepper, and chicken breasts and simmer, partially covered, until just done, about 25 minutes. Turn the chicken breasts a few times during cooking.

2. Meanwhile, in a large pot of boiling, salted water, cook the cavatelli until just done, about 10 minutes. Drain.

3. In a small bowl, stir the butter and flour together to form a paste. Remove the bay leaf from the pot, push the chicken to the side and then whisk the butter mixture into the liquid. Simmer until thickened, 1 to 2 minutes. Stir in the cooked cavatelli and simmer until just heated through.

FROZEN PASTA

Several brands of frozen cavatelli, flat egg noodles, and gnocchi are available in supermarkets. Unlike dried pasta, these products have an appealing doughy chew that we find just right with this type of saucy stew. Cook the frozen pasta separately according to package directions, drain, and then stir into the pot with the chicken.

wine recommendation

Because this dish has no bold or assertive flavors to compete with the wine, options are unlimited: red or white, full-flavored or light-bodied. Three good choices would be a merlot or a chardonnay from California or a Meursault (also made from chardonnay) from France.

chicken thighs with lentils, chorizo, & red pepper

Reminiscent of cassoulet—the glorious goose, sausage, and bean casserole from south-western France—this dish is quick, easy, and bound to become a winter favorite. If you like, use a green bell pepper in place of the red.

PREP TIME 7 MINUTES   **COOK TIME** 30 MINUTES
REST TIME 5 MINUTES
SERVES 4

1²⁄₃ cups lentils (about ²⁄₃ pound)
3 cups water
1 teaspoon salt
¼ teaspoon dried thyme
1 bay leaf
2 tablespoons cooking oil
½ pound dried chorizo or salami, casings removed, cut into ⅛-inch slices
1 onion, chopped
2 cloves garlic, minced
1 red bell pepper, cut into 1-inch pieces
4 chicken thighs
¼ teaspoon fresh-ground black pepper
²⁄₃ cup canned low-sodium chicken broth or homemade stock
2 tablespoons lemon juice
2 tablespoons chopped fresh parsley

1. In a large saucepan, bring the lentils, water, ¾ teaspoon of the salt, the thyme, and bay leaf to a boil over moderately high heat. Reduce the heat. Simmer, covered, until the lentils are tender but not falling apart, about 25 minutes.

2. Meanwhile, in a large frying pan, heat 1 tablespoon of the oil over moderate heat. Add the chorizo and cook, stirring occasionally, until browned, about 5 minutes. Pour off all but 2 tablespoons of the fat from the pan. Reduce the heat to moderately low and add the onion, garlic, and bell pepper. Cook, stirring occasionally, until the onion is translucent, about 5 minutes. Add the onion mixture to the simmering lentils.

3. Heat the remaining tablespoon of oil in the pan over moderate heat. Season the chicken with the remaining ¼ teaspoon salt and the black pepper and add it to the pan. Cook the chicken, turning, until brown, about 12 minutes in all. Pour off all the fat from the pan. Add the broth, reduce the heat and simmer, covered, until the chicken is just done, about 15 minutes. Add the pan juices from the chicken to the lentils along with the lemon juice and the parsley. Top with the chicken and let sit, covered, for 5 minutes.

wine recommendation

The chorizo, pepper, and lentils pair well with a full-flavored, bold red wine. Two possibilities from France: a red from the Médoc, in Bordeaux, or a Châteauneuf-du-Pape from the southern Rhône Valley.

chicken noodle soup with parsnips & dill

Lots of carrots and parsnips give old-favorite chicken noodle soup a sweet savor. To balance this effect, use the optional parsley, which is just slightly bitter.

PREP TIME 10 MINUTES   **COOK TIME** 20 MINUTES

SERVES 4

1½ quarts canned low-sodium chicken broth or homemade stock

1 onion, chopped

4 carrots, halved lengthwise and cut crosswise into 1-inch pieces

4 parsnips, halved lengthwise and cut crosswise into 1-inch pieces

1½ teaspoons salt

¼ teaspoon fresh-ground black pepper

1 pound boneless, skinless chicken breasts (about 3)

1 cup wide egg noodles (about 2 ounces)

¼ cup chopped fresh dill

¼ cup chopped fresh parsley (optional)

1. In a large pot, combine the broth, onion, carrots, parsnips, salt, and pepper and bring to a simmer. Add the chicken to the pot and simmer until just done, about 10 minutes. Remove the chicken; bring the soup back to a simmer. When the chicken breasts are cool enough to handle, cut them into bite-size pieces.

2. Meanwhile, stir the noodles into the soup. Simmer until the vegetables are tender and the noodles are done, about 5 minutes. Return the chicken pieces to the pot and then stir in the dill and the parsley.

VARIATION

Chicken Noodle Soup with Turnips & Dill

Skip the parsnips and raise the number of carrots to eight. Add one diced turnip to the mix. Use bone-in chicken breasts and cook them for an additional 10 minutes. The extra time in the pot will give the soup even more flavor.

wine recommendation

In the past 15 years, sauvignon blancs from New Zealand have burst upon the scene and risen to the top of the sauvignon-blanc heap. Sample their ripe citrus and herb flavors and bracing crispness with this soup and you will know why.

moroccan chicken-&-couscous soup

A mainstay in Morocco, steamed couscous topped with a very liquid stew is undeniably delectable, but not exactly quick. We've found, though, that combining all the ingredients in a soup yields similarly sumptuous results in a much shorter time. The dish is decidedly spicy; if you prefer less heat, just reduce the amount of cayenne.

PREP TIME 8 MINUTES   **COOK TIME** 24 MINUTES

SERVES 4

2	tablespoons cooking oil
1	onion, chopped
1	pound boneless, skinless chicken thighs (about 4), cut into approximately 1½-by-¼-inch strips
¼	teaspoon cayenne
1	teaspoon ground cumin
1¾	teaspoons salt
¼	teaspoon fresh-ground black pepper
1	sweet potato (about ½ pound), peeled and cut into ¾-inch cubes
1	zucchini, quartered lengthwise and cut crosswise into 1-inch pieces
¾	cup tomato puree
1	quart water
2	cups canned low-sodium chicken broth or homemade stock
½	cup couscous
⅓	cup chopped fresh parsley

1. In a large pot, heat the oil over moderate heat. Add the onion and cook, stirring occasionally, until translucent, about 5 minutes.

2. Increase the heat to moderately high. Add the chicken, cayenne, cumin, salt, and pepper to the pot. Cook, stirring occasionally, for 2 minutes.

3. Stir in the sweet potato, zucchini, tomato puree, water, and broth. Bring to a boil. Reduce the heat and simmer, stirring occasionally, until the vegetables are tender, about 10 minutes.

4. Add the couscous to the soup. Simmer for 5 minutes, stirring occasionally. Remove the pot from the heat. Let the soup stand, covered, for 2 minutes, then add the parsley and serve.

wine recommendation

Soup with such a riot of flavors needs a wine that's big but simple. Try a California zinfandel here for its generous, spicy fruit, supple texture, and full body.

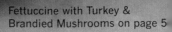

Fettuccine with Turkey &
Brandied Mushrooms on page 5

3

pasta & grains

chicken breasts with orzo, carrots, dill, & avgolemono sauce

Avgolemono sauce, a Greek contribution to the world's cuisine, is a delicate blend of chicken broth, dill, and lemon, thickened lightly with egg. In the spring, asparagus would substitute beautifully for the carrots.

PREP TIME 7 MINUTES   **COOK TIME** 15–18 MINUTES
SERVES 4

2   tablespoons olive oil
4   boneless, skinless chicken breasts
     (about 1⅓ pounds in all)
     Salt and fresh-ground black pepper
1¼ cups canned low-sodium chicken broth
     or homemade stock
1   teaspoon dried dill
1½ cups orzo
4   carrots, quartered and cut into 2-inch lengths
2   eggs
2   tablespoons lemon juice

1. In a large stainless-steel frying pan, heat 1 tablespoon of oil over moderate heat. Season the chicken breasts with ¼ teaspoon salt and ⅛ teaspoon pepper and add to the pan. Cook until browned, about 5 minutes. Turn the chicken; add the broth, dill, and 1¼ teaspoons salt. Bring to a simmer, reduce the heat, and simmer, partially covered, until the chicken is just done, about 4 minutes. Remove the chicken and cover lightly with aluminum foil to keep warm. Set aside the pan with the broth.

2. Meanwhile, in a large pot of boiling, salted water, cook the orzo for 6 minutes. Add the carrots and continue cooking until the orzo and carrots are just done, about 6 minutes longer. Drain and toss with the remaining 1 tablespoon oil and ⅛ teaspoon each salt and pepper.

3. In a medium glass or stainless-steel bowl, beat the eggs, lemon juice, and ⅛ teaspoon of pepper until frothy. Bring the chicken broth back to a simmer and add to the eggs in a thin stream, whisking. Pour the mixture back into the pan and whisk over the lowest possible heat until the sauce begins to thicken, about 3 minutes. Do not let the sauce come to a simmer, or it may curdle. Put the orzo and carrots on plates and top with the chicken and sauce.

wine recommendation
Lemon and dill will work best with a full-flavored white wine with decent acidity. Try one from the southern part of Burgundy, such as a Mâcon or Pouilly-Fuissé (both made from chardonnay grapes).

orecchiette with chicken, caramelized onions, & blue cheese

The sweetness of the onions contrasts perfectly with the saltiness of the cheese in this exciting dish. Orecchiette ("little ears") is a thick and satisfying pasta that we adore, but if you like, you can use shells or bow ties instead.

PREP TIME 6 MINUTES **COOK TIME** 35 MINUTES
STEAMING TIME 5 MINUTES
SERVES 4

1	tablespoon butter
3	tablespoons olive oil
2	onions, quartered and cut into thin slices
1	teaspoon salt
1⅓	pounds boneless, skinless chicken breasts (about 4)
¼	teaspoon fresh-ground black pepper
¾	teaspoon dried rosemary, crumbled, or 2 teaspoons chopped fresh rosemary
1	clove garlic, minced
½	pound orecchiette
2	ounces blue cheese, crumbled (about ½ cup)

1. In a large nonstick frying pan, melt the butter with 2 tablespoons of oil over moderately high heat. Add the onions and ½ teaspoon of the salt and cook, stirring frequently, until well browned, about 25 minutes. Remove.

2. Add the remaining 1 tablespoon oil to the pan and reduce the heat to moderate. Season the chicken with ¼ teaspoon of the salt and ⅛ teaspoon of the pepper and add to the pan along with the rosemary. Cook the chicken until brown, about 5 minutes. Turn and cook until almost done, about 3 minutes longer. Add the garlic. Cook, stirring, for 30 seconds. Cover the pan, remove from the heat, and let steam for 5 minutes. Cut the chicken into ¼-inch slices.

3. Meanwhile, in a large pot of boiling, salted water, cook the orecchiette until just done, about 15 minutes. Reserve about ¼ cup of the pasta water. Drain the pasta and toss with 2 tablespoons of the pasta water, the onions, the chicken with pan juices, the blue cheese, and the remaining ¼ teaspoon salt and ⅛ teaspoon pepper. If the pasta seems dry, add more of the reserved pasta water.

wine recommendation

The onions and cheese drive the wine choice for this dish. A lighter red wine from the Piedmont region of Italy, such as one based on the barbera or dolcetto grapes, has the weight and acidity to stand up to the sweet and salty flavors.

fusilli with spicy chicken sausage, tomato, & ricotta cheese

Hearty and comforting, this pasta makes a great meal for a cold winter evening. If you like, replace the hot sausages with mild ones, or use turkey sausage instead.

PREP TIME 5 MINUTES   **COOK TIME** 30 MINUTES
SERVES 4

1	tablespoon olive oil
1	pound hot chicken sausage
1	onion, chopped
2	cloves garlic, chopped
¼	cup dry white wine
1½	cups canned crushed tomatoes in thick puree
¼	cup water
¼	teaspoon dried rosemary, crumbled
	Pinch dried red-pepper flakes
½	teaspoon salt
3	tablespoons chopped flat-leaf parsley
½	pound fusilli
¾	cup ricotta cheese

1. In a large, deep frying pan, heat the oil over moderate heat. Add the sausage and cook, turning, until browned and cooked through, about 10 minutes. Remove the sausage and, when it is cool enough to handle, cut it into ¼-inch slices. Pour off all but 1 tablespoon fat from the pan.

2. Reduce the heat to moderately low. Add the onion to the pan and cook, stirring occasionally, until translucent, about 5 minutes. Add the garlic and cook 30 seconds longer.

3. Add the wine and bring to a simmer. Add the sausage, tomatoes, water, rosemary, red-pepper flakes, and ¼ teaspoon of the salt and bring to a simmer. Cook, stirring occasionally, for 10 minutes. Stir in the parsley.

4. Meanwhile, in a large pot of boiling, salted water, cook the fusilli until just done, about 13 minutes. Drain and toss with the sauce, the ricotta, and the remaining ¼ teaspoon salt.

wine recommendation

The acidity of the tomato and spiciness of the sausage are best suited to a red wine with soft tannin and good acidity. Try a sangiovese from Tuscany such as Chianti Classico or Rosso di Montalcino or look for a version from California.

chicken pad thai

Our version of pad Thai, the satisfying rice-noodle dish from Thailand, is made with chicken, tofu, bean sprouts, and, in place of rice noodles, linguine. The fish sauce is available at Asian markets and keeps forever. If you like, you can use a mixture of soy sauce and oyster sauce instead. Lime wedges make a nice final touch.

PREP TIME 10 MINUTES   **COOK TIME** 12–15 MINUTES
SERVES 4

1	pound boneless, skinless chicken breasts (about 3), cut into 1-inch cubes
5	tablespoons plus 1 teaspoon Asian fish sauce
½	pound firm tofu, cut into ¼-inch cubes
1	cup water
2	tablespoons lime juice
1½	teaspoons rice-wine vinegar
3½	tablespoons sugar
¾	teaspoon salt
¼	teaspoon cayenne
¾	pound linguine
3	tablespoons cooking oil
4	cloves garlic, chopped
⅔	cup salted peanuts, chopped fine
2	cups bean sprouts
½	cup lightly packed cilantro leaves

1. In a small bowl, combine the chicken and ½ teaspoon of the fish sauce. In another bowl, combine the tofu with another ½ teaspoon of the fish sauce. In a medium glass or stainless-steel bowl, combine the remaining 5 tablespoons fish sauce with the water, 1½ tablespoons of the lime juice, the vinegar, sugar, salt, and cayenne.

2. In a pot of boiling, salted water, cook the linguine until done, about 12 minutes. Drain.

3. Meanwhile, in a work or large frying pan, heat 1 tablespoon of the oil over moderately high heat. Add the chicken and cook, stirring, until just done, 3 to 4 minutes. Remove. Put another tablespoon of oil in the pan. Add the tofu and cook, stirring, for 2 minutes. Remove. Put the remaining 1 tablespoon oil in the pan, add the garlic and cook, stirring, for 30 seconds.

4. Add the pasta and the fish-sauce mixture. Cook, stirring, until nearly all the liquid is absorbed, about 3 minutes. Stir in the chicken, tofu, and ⅓ cup peanuts. Remove from the heat. Stir in the remaining ½ tablespoon lime juice, the bean sprouts, and half the cilantro. Top with the remaining peanuts and cilantro.

wine recommendation

Anything more than a straightforward white with some residual sugar would be pointless with the forceful flavors of the pad Thai. A riesling from California or Australia will be fine.

fettuccine with turkey & brandied mushrooms

A hint of brandy flavors the sautéed mushrooms. You could also use port or sherry. For a special treat, try an assortment of wild mushrooms.

PREP TIME 8 MINUTES   **COOK TIME** 15 MINUTES

SERVES 4

1	tablespoon cooking oil
1	pound turkey cutlets (about 3)
1¼	teaspoons salt
½	teaspoon fresh-ground black pepper
2	tablespoons butter
2	scallions, white bulbs and green tops chopped separately
1	pound mushrooms, cut into thin slices
⅓	cup brandy
1	cup canned low-sodium chicken broth or homemade stock
½	pound fettuccine
¼	cup heavy cream
2	tablespoons chopped fresh parsley

1. In a large nonstick frying pan, heat the oil over moderately high heat. Season the turkey cutlets with ¼ teaspoon each of the salt and pepper. Cook the cutlets until they are almost done, about 1 minute per side. Remove the cutlets from the pan, let cool, and then cut them into thin strips.

2. Melt the butter in the same pan over moderate heat. Add the white part of the scallions, the mushrooms, ½ teaspoon of the salt, and the remaining ¼ teaspoon pepper. Cook, stirring occasionally, until the mushrooms let off their liquid and it evaporates, about 5 minutes. Add the brandy and cook until almost no liquid remains in the pan, about 2 minutes more. Add ½ cup of broth and simmer until almost completely evaporated, about 4 minutes.

3. In a large pot of boiling, salted water, cook the fettuccine until almost done, about 7 minutes. Drain the pasta and then add it to the mushrooms. Add the remaining ½ cup broth, the cream, the scallion tops, the remaining ½ teaspoon salt, and the turkey strips. Simmer until the turkey is just done, about 1 minute longer. Top with the parsley.

MENU SUGGESTION

A simple side dish of steamed or sautéed green beans is all that's needed.

wine recommendation

The sweetness here will be nicely mirrored by an off-dry, aromatic white wine, such as a chenin blanc, riesling, or gewürztraminer from California.

chicken & zucchini couscous

A version of the North African classic, this recipe combines chicken, chickpeas, and zucchini in a cumin-spiced tomato broth. Traditionally chicken is braised in a special pot with a top compartment for steaming the couscous, but you can cook couscous, available at most supermarkets, in a saucepan in a matter of minutes.

PREP TIME 6 MINUTES   **COOK TIME** 35 MINUTES
SERVES 4

1	tablespoon olive oil
1	chicken (3 to 3½ pounds), cut into 8 pieces
1½	teaspoons salt
1	onion, chopped
4	cloves garlic, chopped
1	tablespoon chopped fresh ginger
½	teaspoon paprika
¾	teaspoon ground cumin
½	teaspoon dried oregano
¼	teaspoon cayenne
¼	teaspoon ground turmeric
1½	cups canned low-sodium chicken broth or homemade stock
1	cup canned crushed tomatoes in thick puree
1	cup canned chickpeas, drained and rinsed
1	zucchini, cut into ¼-inch slices
3	tablespoons chopped fresh parsley
1	tablespoon lemon juice
4	cups cooked couscous

1. In a large pot, heat the oil over moderately high heat. Season the chicken pieces with ¼ teaspoon of the salt and add them to the pot. Cook, turning, until browned, about 8 minutes in all. Remove. Pour off all but 1 tablespoon fat from the pot.

2. Reduce the heat to moderately low. Add the onion to the pot and cook, stirring occasionally, until translucent, about 5 minutes. Add the garlic, ginger, paprika, cumin, oregano, cayenne, and turmeric and cook, stirring, for 30 seconds.

3. Add the broth, tomatoes, and the remaining 1¼ teaspoons of salt, scraping the bottom of the pot to dislodge any browned bits. Add the chicken thighs and drumsticks. Bring to a simmer and cook, covered, for 10 minutes. Add the chicken breasts with any accumulated juices, the chickpeas, and the zucchini and bring back to a simmer. Cook, covered, until the chicken and zucchini are just done, about 12 minutes longer. Add the parsley and lemon juice and serve over the couscous.

wine recommendation

The aromatic spices in this dish are best with an assertive, flavorful wine; color is almost secondary. For a red, try a wine from the indigenous South African grape, pinotage. For white, try a Tokay Pinot Gris from Alsace in France.

mushroom & chicken risotto

If you're using canned chicken broth to make risotto, be sure it's low-sodium. The broth reduces at the same time that it's cooking into the rice, and regular canned broth would become much too salty.

PREP TIME 6 MINUTES   **COOK TIME** 45–50 MINUTES
SERVES 4

2	tablespoons butter
½	pound mushrooms, cut into thin slices
⅔	pound boneless, skinless chicken breasts (about 2), cut into ½-inch pieces
1	teaspoon salt
¼	teaspoon fresh-ground black pepper
5½	cups canned low-sodium chicken broth or homemade stock, more if needed
1	tablespoon cooking oil
½	cup chopped onion
1½	cups arborio rice
½	cup dry white wine
½	cup grated Parmesan cheese, plus more for serving
2	tablespoons chopped fresh parsley

1. In a large pot, heat the butter over moderate heat. Add the mushrooms. Cook, stirring frequently, until the mushrooms are browned, about 5 minutes. Add the chicken, ¼ teaspoon of the salt, and the pepper. Cook until the chicken is just done, 3 to 4 minutes. Remove the mixture from the pan. In a medium saucepan, bring the broth to a simmer.

2. In the large pot, heat the oil over moderately low heat. Add the onion and cook, stirring occasionally, until translucent, about 5 minutes. Add the rice and stir until it begins to turn opaque, about 2 minutes.

3. Add the wine and the remaining ¾ teaspoon salt to the rice. Cook, stirring frequently, until all of the wine has been absorbed. Add about ½ cup of the simmering broth and cook, stirring frequently, until it has been absorbed. The rice and broth should bubble gently; adjust the heat as needed. Continue cooking the rice, adding broth ½ cup at a time and allowing the rice to absorb it before adding the next ½ cup. Cook the rice in this way until tender, 25 to 30 minutes in all. The broth that hasn't been absorbed should be thickened by the starch from the rice. You may not need to use all the liquid, or you may need more broth or some water.

4. Stir in the chicken and mushrooms, the Parmesan, and the parsley and heat through. Serve the risotto with additional Parmesan.

wine recommendation

The sweetness here will be nicely mirrored by an off-dry, aromatic white wine, such as a chenin blanc, riesling, or gewürztraminer from California.

risotto with smoked turkey, leeks, & mascarpone

The mascarpone gives this risotto its delectable creaminess. If you like, you can make a close substitute with 2 ounces of cream cheese, at room temperature, and 7 ounces of heavy cream. Whir them in a blender just until smooth; don't blend the mixture too long or it may curdle. Also, you can use a large onion in place of the leeks.

PREP TIME 5 MINUTES   **COOK TIME** 45–50 MINUTES
SERVES 4

5	cups canned low-sodium chicken broth or homemade stock, more if needed
1	cup water, more if needed
3	tablespoons olive oil
1½	pounds leeks (about 3), white and light-green parts only, cut crosswise into thin slices and washed well
2	cups arborio rice
½	cup dry white wine
2	teaspoons salt
1	6-ounce piece smoked turkey, cut into ¼-inch dice
1	cup mascarpone cheese
¼	teaspoon fresh-ground black pepper

1. In a medium saucepan, bring the chicken broth and water to a simmer.

2. In a large pot, heat the oil over moderately low heat. Add the leeks and cook, stirring occasionally, until translucent, about 10 minutes. Add the rice and stir until it begins to turn opaque, about 2 minutes.

3. Add the wine and salt to the rice and cook, stirring frequently, until all of the wine has been absorbed.

4. Add about ½ cup of the simmering broth to the rice and cook, stirring frequently, until the broth has been completely absorbed. The rice and broth should bubble gently; adjust the heat as needed. Continue cooking the rice, adding the broth ½ cup at a time and allowing the rice to absorb the stock before adding the next ½ cup. Cook the rice in this way until tender, 25 to 30 minutes in all. The broth that hasn't been absorbed should be thickened by the starch from the rice. You may not need to use all of the liquid, or you may need to add more broth or water. Stir in the turkey, cheese, and pepper.

wine recommendation

Go for an Italian white wine with good body and acidity to offset the creaminess here. Look for an Arneis from the Piedmont region or a pinot grigio either from the region of Alto Adige or Collio.

arroz con pollo

Here's a perfect all-in-one meal—the chicken, rice, and vegetables simmer together, enhancing each other and giving the cook a break.

PREP TIME 10 MINUTES   **COOK TIME** 40 MINUTES
SERVES 4

1	tablespoon olive oil
4	chicken thighs
4	chicken drumsticks
2	teaspoons salt
½	teaspoon fresh-ground black pepper
2	ounces smoked ham, cut into ¼-inch dice
1	small onion, chopped
2	cloves garlic, minced
1	red bell pepper, chopped
1	green bell pepper, chopped
1¾	cups canned tomatoes, drained and chopped
1	tablespoon tomato paste
2	cups canned low-sodium chicken broth or homemade stock
1	cup rice, preferably long-grain
2	tablespoons chopped fresh parsley

1. In a large, deep frying pan, heat the oil over moderately high heat. Season the chicken with ¼ teaspoon each of the salt and pepper. Cook the chicken, turning, until well browned, about 8 minutes in all. Remove. Pour off all but 2 tablespoons of the fat from the pan.

2. Reduce the heat to moderately low. Add the ham, onion, and garlic to the pan and cook, stirring occasionally, until the onion starts to soften, about 2 minutes. Add the bell peppers and cook, stirring occasionally, until they start to soften, about 3 minutes longer.

3. Add the tomatoes, tomato paste, broth, and the remaining 1¾ teaspoons salt and ¼ teaspoon of the pepper and bring to a simmer. Stir in the rice and add the chicken in an even layer. Simmer, partially covered, over moderately low heat until the chicken and rice are just done, 20 to 25 minutes. Sprinkle with parsley.

wine recommendation

This traditional Spanish favorite will work well with any smooth, full-flavored red, such as a merlot or zinfandel from California or a Rioja from Spain.

chicken with rice & beans

Three favorite Latin-American ingredients combine here to make one hearty and delicious dish that's welcome any time of year. We recommend Goya® canned black beans, which hold up during cooking better than other brands do.

PREP TIME 10 MINUTES   **COOK TIME** 40–45 MINUTES
SERVES 4

1	tablespoon cooking oil
4	chicken thighs
4	chicken drumsticks
1¾	teaspoons salt
¼	teaspoon fresh-ground black pepper
1	onion, chopped fine
2	cloves garlic, minced
1	cup canned crushed tomatoes
½	cup bottled pimientos, drained
1⅔	cups drained and rinsed black beans (from one 15-ounce can)
1	cup rice, preferably medium-grain
1¾	cups water
2	tablespoons chopped fresh parsley
⅛	teaspoon cayenne
4	lime wedges (optional)

1. In a large, deep frying pan, heat the oil over moderately high heat. Season the chicken with ¼ teaspoon of the salt and the pepper and add to the pan. Cook, turning, until well browned, about 8 minutes in all. Remove. Pour off all but 1 tablespoon of the fat from the pan.

2. Add the onion to the pan and reduce the heat to moderately low. Cook, stirring occasionally, until translucent, about 5 minutes. Add the garlic and cook, stirring, for 30 seconds longer. Add the tomatoes and pimientos, scraping the bottom of the pan to dislodge any brown bits. Stir in the beans, rice, water, parsley, the remaining 1½ teaspoons of salt, and the cayenne. Arrange the chicken on top in an even layer.

3. Bring to a boil and simmer until all the water is absorbed, about 12 minutes. Turn the drumsticks and reduce the heat to very low. Cover and cook until the chicken and rice are just done, about 15 minutes longer. Serve with the lime wedges, if using.

wine recommendation

A fruity red wine such as a merlot is best with this classic dish. If you can, try to find a bottle from Argentina or Chile, or open your favorite California merlot.

turkey sausage with cheddar-cheese grits & tomato sauce

Creamy, cheesy grits capture the juices from the fresh tomatoes, making a perfect foil for the sausage links. Chicken sausage also works well in this homey combination.

PREP TIME 5 MINUTES   **COOK TIME** 20–25 MINUTES
SERVES 4

3½ cups water
1   teaspoon salt
¾   cup old-fashioned grits
¼   pound cheddar cheese, grated
1   tablespoon cooking oil
1   pound turkey sausages
1½ pounds tomatoes, chopped (about 2 cups)
¼   teaspoon fresh-ground black pepper
2   tablespoons chopped fresh parsley

1. In a medium saucepan, bring the water and ¾ teaspoon salt to a boil. Add the grits in a slow stream, whisking. Reduce the heat, cover, and simmer, stirring frequently with a wooden spoon, until the grits are very thick, about 20 minutes. Remove the saucepan from the heat and stir in the cheese.

2. Meanwhile, in a medium, nonstick frying pan, heat the oil over moderately low heat. Add the sausages and cook until they are just done, about 15 minutes. Remove the sausages from the pan. Add the tomatoes, the remaining ¼ teaspoon salt, and the pepper to the pan. Cook until the tomatoes are just heated through, 1 to 2 minutes. Stir in the parsley.

3. Serve the grits topped with the sausages and the tomato sauce.

MENU SUGGESTIONS
Vegetables such as okra, lima beans, or cooked greens would be perfectly in keeping with the Southern theme.

wine recommendation

A simple, refreshing white wine is a nice contrast to the rich cheddar flavor of the grits. Try a pinot bianco from the Veneto region of Italy or a pinot blanc from Alsace in France.

grilled-chicken pasta salad with artichoke hearts

Using canned artichoke hearts cuts the preparation time for this salad way down. They are surprisingly good; just be sure to rinse them thoroughly to get rid of any extra acidity or "tinny" taste.

PREP TIME 6 MINUTES   **COOK TIME** 15 MINUTES
REST TIME 5 MINUTES
SERVES 4

3   boneless, skinless chicken breasts (about 1 pound in all)
7   tablespoons olive oil
1¼   teaspoons salt
½   teaspoon fresh-ground black pepper
¾   pound fusilli
1¼   cups canned, drained artichoke hearts (one 14-ounce can), rinsed and cut into 6 wedges each
3   scallions including green tops, chopped
¼   cup chopped flat-leaf parsley
1   tablespoon red-wine vinegar
2   tablespoons grated Parmesan cheese

1. Light the grill or heat the broiler. Coat the chicken with 1 tablespoon of the oil and season with ¼ teaspoon of the salt and ¼ teaspoon of the pepper. Grill or broil until just done, 4 to 5 minutes per side. Let the chicken rest for 5 minutes and then cut crosswise into ¼-inch slices.

2. In a large pot of boiling, salted water, cook the fusilli until just done, about 13 minutes. Drain, rinse with cold water, and drain thoroughly. In a large bowl, toss the pasta with 1 tablespoon of the olive oil.

3. Add the chicken, artichoke hearts, scallions, parsley, the remaining 5 tablespoons oil, the vinegar, the remaining 1 teaspoon salt and ¼ teaspoon pepper, and the Parmesan to the pasta and toss well.

wine recommendation

Artichokes can be tough on wine since they tend to make even the driest ones taste sweet. To counteract this tendency, try an acidic white wine such as a Sancerre from France (made from sauvignon blanc grapes) or a sauvignon blanc from northern Italy.

pasta shells with chicken & brussels sprouts

If you've always thought that you dislike Brussels sprouts, you've probably never tried them in a combination like this. Mild chicken tames the strength of the sprouts while garlic, lemon juice, red-pepper flakes, and Parmesan unite the two main ingredients and complement them both. Frozen Brussels sprouts are surprisingly good in this recipe, too, though not as fine as fresh.

PREP TIME 8 MINUTES   **COOK TIME** 20 MINUTES

REST TIME 5 MINUTES

SERVES 4

2	tablespoons cooking oil
3	tablespoons butter
4	boneless, skinless chicken breasts (about 1⅓ pounds in all)
1	teaspoon salt
½	teaspoon fresh-ground black pepper
½	red onion, chopped
2	cloves garlic, chopped
¾	pound fresh Brussels sprouts (or a 10-ounce package frozen), cut into quarters from top to stem end
1	cup canned low-sodium chicken broth or homemade stock
⅛	teaspoon dried red-pepper flakes
1½	teaspoons lemon juice
¼	cup chopped fresh parsley
⅓	cup grated Parmesan cheese
½	pound medium pasta shells

1. In a large nonstick frying pan, heat 1 tablespoon each of the oil and the butter over moderate heat. Season the chicken breasts with ¼ teaspoon each of the salt and pepper. Cook the chicken until browned and just done, 4 to 5 minutes per side. Remove the chicken from the pan and let it rest for 5 minutes. Cut into small pieces.

2. In the same pan, heat the remaining 1 tablespoon oil over moderately low heat. Add the red onion and cook, stirring occasionally, until starting to soften, about 3 minutes. Stir in the garlic, Brussels sprouts, broth, and red-pepper flakes. Bring to a simmer and cook, covered, until the Brussels sprouts are just done, about 5 minutes. Add the chicken, lemon juice, parsley, Parmesan, and the remaining 2 tablespoons butter, ¾ teaspoon salt, and ¼ teaspoon pepper. Remove from the heat.

3. Meanwhile, in a large pot of boiling, salted water, cook the pasta until just done, about 10 minutes. Drain and toss with the sauce.

wine recommendation

A crisp white wine such as a chardonnay-based Chablis from France matches up nicely with the acidity of the lemon juice in the sauce.

penne with turkey, arugula, & sun-dried tomato vinaigrette

Peppery arugula adds a distinctive bite to this appealing dish, but if arugula is unavailable, you can substitute watercress with similar results.

PREP TIME 8 MINUTES   **COOK TIME** 15 MINUTES
SERVES 4

6	reconstituted sun-dried tomato halves, chopped (see "Reconstituting Sun-Dried Tomatoes," page 116)
2	cloves garlic, smashed
1½	tablespoons balsamic vinegar
¾	teaspoon salt
½	teaspoon fresh-ground black pepper
⅓	cup plus 1 tablespoon olive oil
1	pound turkey cutlets, cut into ½-by-1 ½-inch strips
6	ounces arugula (about 3 bunches), cut into ½-inch strips, or 5 ounces (1 bunch) watercress, large stems removed
½	pound penne

1. In a blender, combine the sun-dried tomatoes, garlic, vinegar, ½ teaspoon of the salt, and ¼ teaspoon of the pepper. Blend until a paste forms. With the machine running, add the ⅓ cup oil in a thin stream.

2. Sprinkle the turkey with the remaining ¼ teaspoon each of the salt and pepper. In a large frying pan, heat the remaining 1 tablespoon oil over moderate heat. Cook the turkey, in two batches if necessary, until just cooked through, about 3 minutes. Do not overcook. Transfer the turkey to a large bowl and add the arugula.

3. In a large pot of boiling, salted water, cook the penne until just done, about 13 minutes. Drain, toss with the turkey and arugula and the tomato vinaigrette, and serve warm.

wine recommendation

A fruity red will complement the sharpness of the arugula. Try a Beaujolais-Villages from France or a dolcetto from Italy. In either case, chill the wine slightly before serving.

Chicken with Wine & Tarragon
on page 86.

roasted, baked, & grilled

roast chicken with rosemary & lemon

Lemon zest and rosemary placed in the cavity of the bird permeate the meat as it cooks and give a subtle Mediterranean accent to the pan juices. We call for dried rosemary, but if you have fresh, use several sprigs in place of the 1 tablespoon.

PREP TIME 5 MINUTES   **ROAST TIME** 1 HOUR
SERVES 4

1	chicken (3 to 3 ½ pounds)
1	tablespoon dried rosemary
	Salt
	Fresh-ground black pepper
4	3-inch-long strips lemon zest
1	small onion, quartered
1	tablespoon olive oil
1	tablespoon plus ¼ teaspoon lemon juice
½	cup water

1. Heat the oven to 425°. Rub the cavity of the chicken with the dried rosemary, ¼ teaspoon salt, and ⅛ teaspoon pepper and then stuff with the strips of lemon zest and the quartered onion. Twist the wings behind the back of the chicken and tie the legs together. Put the chicken, breast-side up, in a roasting pan. Coat the chicken with the oil and sprinkle it with ¼ teaspoon of salt, ⅛ teaspoon of pepper, and the 1 tablespoon lemon juice.

2. Roast the chicken until it is just done, 50 to 60 minutes. Transfer the bird to a plate and leave to rest in a warm spot for about 10 minutes.

3. Meanwhile, pour off the fat from the roasting pan. Set the pan over moderate heat and add the water. Bring to a boil, scraping the bottom of the pan to dislodge any brown bits. Boil until reduced to approximately ¼ cup, about 4 minutes. Add any accumulated juices from the chicken along with the remaining ¼ teaspoon lemon juice and a pinch each of salt and pepper. Serve the bird with the pan juices.

MENU SUGGESTIONS
The simplicity of this chicken means that an almost endless list of accompaniments will work well with it. Among the easiest are vegetables that you can roast in a separate pan alongside the chicken, such as potatoes, squash, asparagus, or fennel. Other good choices include rice, polenta, or mashed potatoes.

wine recommendation
A straightforward gulpable red wine will pair best with this aromatic dish. Try a Chianti from the Italian region of Tuscany.

roast chicken with cranberry-apple-raisin chutney

Cranberries may call the holidays to mind, but this combination tastes great any time of year. You can serve the chutney warm or at room temperature; if there's any left over, use it to light up a chicken, turkey, or ham sandwich.

PREP TIME 6 MINUTES   **COOK TIME** 65 MINUTES
REST TIME 10 MINUTES
SERVES 4

1   chicken (3 to 3 ½ pounds)
     Salt
     Fresh-ground black pepper
4   3-inch-long strips orange zest
1   tablespoon olive oil
1   12-ounce package fresh or frozen cranberries
     (about 3 cups)
1   tart apple, such as Granny Smith, peeled, cored,
     and cut into ½-inch chunks
1   cup raisins
⅔   cup brown sugar
½   cup apple juice
4   teaspoons cider vinegar
¼   teaspoon ground ginger
½   cup orange juice (from about 1 orange)

1. Heat the oven to 425°. Rub the chicken cavity with ¼ teaspoon salt and ⅛ teaspoon pepper and put the orange zest inside. Twist the wings of the chicken behind the back and tie the legs together. Put the chicken, breast-side up, in a roasting pan. Coat the chicken with the oil and sprinkle with ¼ teaspoon salt and ⅛ teaspoon pepper. Roast the chicken until just done, 50 to 60 minutes.

2. Meanwhile, in a medium stainless-steel saucepan, bring the cranberries to a boil with the apple, raisins, brown sugar, apple juice, vinegar, ginger, ⅛ teaspoon salt, and ⅛ teaspoon pepper. Cover and simmer over moderate heat, stirring occasionally, until the liquid has thickened and the fruit is tender, about 15 minutes.

3. When the chicken is done, transfer the bird to a plate and leave to rest in a warm spot for about 10 minutes. Pour off the fat from the roasting pan. Set the pan over moderate heat and add the orange juice. Bring to a boil, scraping the bottom of the pan to dislodge any brown bits. Boil until reduced to approximately ¼ cup, about 4 minutes. Add any accumulated juices from the chicken and a pinch each of salt and pepper. Serve the chicken with the orange sauce and the chutney.

wine recommendation
This sweet, fruit-laden dish is best with a wine that shares these characteristics, such as a slightly chilled bottle of Chinon from the Loire Valley in France or a dolcetto from Italy.

roast chicken with maple-pepper glaze & sweet potatoes

You'll look forward to cool weather just so you can make this irresistible dish. The maple-pepper glaze laced with bourbon gives the chicken an extra-crisp skin and drips down to flavor the sweet potatoes as they roast alongside. To gild the lily, add 1 cup of pecan halves to the potatoes about 10 minutes before they're done.

PREP TIME 5 MINUTES   **ROAST TIME** 1 HOUR
REST TIME 10 MINUTES
SERVES 4

2   pounds sweet potatoes (about 3), peeled and cut into 1½-inch pieces
2   tablespoons cooking oil
1   teaspoon salt
1¼ teaspoons fresh-ground black pepper
1   chicken (3 to 3½ pounds)
1   tablespoon butter, cut into small pieces
6   tablespoons pure maple syrup
1½ tablespoons bourbon

1. Heat the oven to 425°. In a large roasting pan, toss the sweet potatoes with 1 tablespoon of the oil, ½ teaspoon of the salt, and ¼ teaspoon of the pepper. Push them to the edges of the pan, leaving a space in the center for the chicken.

2. Rub the cavity of the chicken with ¼ teaspoon of the salt and ⅛ teaspoon of the pepper. Twist the wings behind the back and tie the legs together. Put the chicken, breast-side up, in the center of the roasting pan. Coat the chicken with the remaining tablespoon oil, sprinkle with the remaining ¼ teaspoon salt and ⅛ teaspoon of the pepper, and dot with the butter. Roast the chicken for 30 minutes.

3. Meanwhile, in a small bowl, combine the maple syrup, bourbon, and the remaining ¾ teaspoon pepper. Remove the roasting pan from the oven and stir the potatoes. Brush the chicken with about 2 tablespoons of the glaze and drizzle the potatoes with about ½ tablespoon of the glaze. Return the pan to the oven and cook, stirring the potatoes and brushing the chicken with the remaining glaze 2 more times, until the chicken and potatoes are just done, about 30 minutes longer. Transfer the bird and potatoes to a plate and leave to rest in a warm spot for about 10 minutes.

4. Meanwhile, pour off the fat from the roasting pan. Add any accumulated juices from the chicken to the liquid in the pan. Serve the chicken with the pan juices and sweet potatoes.

wine recommendation

With ingredients like maple syrup, bourbon, and sweet potatoes, this dish should be matched with an all-American wine. The best choice is a fruity zinfandel from California.

roast cornish hens with panzanella stuffing

Italian bread salad is the inspiration for this simple stuffing that bakes in a dish alongside the hens until crisp and golden brown.

PREP TIME 6 MINUTES   **COOK TIME** 40 MINUTES
REST TIME 10 MINUTES
SERVES 4

1	½-pound loaf sourdough or firm country bread, cut into 1-inch cubes (about 8 cups)
2	Cornish hens
3	tablespoons olive oil
1	teaspoon salt
	Fresh-ground black pepper
1	tablespoon butter, cut into small pieces
2	cups drained diced canned tomatoes
3	cloves garlic, minced
6	tablespoons chopped flat-leaf parsley
2	teaspoons dried rosemary, crumbled, or 2 tablespoons chopped fresh rosemary

1. Set the oven at 425°. Put the bread cubes in the oven while it heats and toast them until golden brown, about 6 minutes.

2. Twist the wings of the Cornish hens behind their backs and tie the legs together. Put the hens, breast-side up, in a roasting pan. Coat the hens with 1 tablespoon of the oil; sprinkle with ¼ teaspoon of the salt and ⅛ teaspoon pepper. Dot with the butter. Roast the hens until just done, about 40 minutes.

3. Meanwhile, oil a deep 1-quart baking dish. In a large bowl, toss the tomatoes with the garlic, parsley, rosemary, the remaining ¾ teaspoon salt, and ¼ teaspoon pepper. Add the toasted bread cubes and the remaining 2 tablespoons oil and stir well to combine. Put the stuffing in the prepared baking dish and cover with a lid or with aluminum foil. Bake for 20 minutes. Remove the cover; bake until the stuffing is crisp and golden brown, about 12 minutes longer.

4. When the hens are done, transfer them to a plate and leave to rest in a warm spot for about 10 minutes. Pour off the fat from the roasting pan and add any accumulated juices from the hens to the serving plate. Cut the hens in half and serve with the stuffing and the pan juices.

MENU SUGGESTION
Only a green vegetable, perhaps broccoli rabe, is needed to complete the meal.

wine recommendation

This rustic, Italian-influenced recipe will go nicely with an Italian red such as a Chianti Classico. It combines fruit flavors with enough acidity to stand up to the strong ingredients here.

turkey breast with mustard-sage crumbs

Seasoned bread crumbs form an appealing brown crust on this turkey breast that looks as good as it tastes. We developed it for quick weeknight cooking, but it would make a fine holiday feast for a small group.

PREP TIME 5 MINUTES   **COOK TIME** 40 MINUTES
REST TIME 10 MINUTES
SERVES 4

½   cup dry bread crumbs
1½   teaspoons dried sage
¼   cup chopped fresh parsley
3   tablespoons melted butter
¾   teaspoon salt
1   2-pound boneless, skinless turkey breast
¼   teaspoon fresh-ground black pepper
1   tablespoon Dijon mustard

1. Heat the oven to 450°. In a small bowl, combine the bread crumbs, sage, parsley, butter, and ¼ teaspoon of the salt.

2. Season the turkey breast with the remaining ½ teaspoon salt and the pepper. Set the turkey breast in a roasting pan and then brush the top and the sides of the breast with the mustard. Pat the seasoned bread crumbs onto the mustard.

3. Roast the turkey breast for 20 minutes. Reduce the oven temperature to 375° and continue to roast the turkey breast until just done, 15 to 20 minutes longer. Transfer the turkey breast to a carving board and leave to rest in a warm spot for about 10 minutes. Cut the turkey breast into slices.

MENU SUGGESTIONS
A creamy side dish—mashed potatoes or sweet potatoes, baked squash, or creamed corn or spinach—is the perfect foil for the turkey.

TEST-KITCHEN TIP
Sometimes boneless turkey breasts come rolled and tied like a roast. For this preparation, you'll want to unroll the breast and put it flat in the roasting pan, thereby cutting the cooking time significantly.

wine recommendation

The mild flavors of this dish provide an opportunity to explore a full-flavored red wine. Try a bottle of easy-to-like, easy-to-drink zinfandel from California or a shiraz from Australia.

chicken with wine & tarragon

Here's a delectable French classic that never seems to go out of style. The sauce takes only a few minutes to make, but if you prefer you can serve the chicken without it. Green beans are a good accompaniment.

PREP TIME 3 MINUTES   **COOK TIME** 40 MINUTES
SERVES 4

3   tablespoons dry white wine or dry vermouth
2   teaspoons dried tarragon
1   chicken (3 to 3½ pounds), quartered
1   tablespoon olive oil
     Salt
     Fresh-ground black pepper
1   tablespoon butter, cut into 4 pieces
¼   cup water

1. Heat the oven to 375°. In a small glass or stainless-steel bowl, combine 2 tablespoons of the wine and ½ teaspoon of the tarragon. Set aside.

2. Coat the chicken with the olive oil and arrange the pieces, skin-side up, in a large roasting pan. Sprinkle the chicken pieces with the remaining 1 tablespoon wine and season with ¼ teaspoon salt and ⅛ teaspoon pepper. Top each piece of chicken with a piece of the butter.

3. Cook the chicken for 15 minutes and then sprinkle with the remaining 1½ teaspoons tarragon. Baste the chicken and cook until the breasts are just done, about 20 minutes longer. Remove the breasts and cook the legs until done, about 5 minutes longer. Remove the roasting pan from the oven; return the breasts to the pan.

4. Heat the broiler. Baste the chicken and then broil until the skin is golden brown, about 2 minutes. Transfer the chicken to a plate.

5. Pour off the fat from the roasting pan. Set the pan over moderate heat and add the reserved wine-and-tarragon mixture and the water. Bring to a boil, scraping the bottom of the pan to dislodge any brown bits. Boil until reduced to approximately 3 tablespoons, about 3 minutes. Add any accumulated juices from the chicken and a pinch each of salt and pepper. Spoon the sauce over the chicken.

wine recommendation

A full-bodied, rustic red wine from the south of France is a perfect choice for this traditional French dish. A Gigondas, Côtes-du-Rhône, or Crozes-Hermitage, each from the Rhône Valley, would be a good choice.

chicken with port & figs

Dried figs are poached in port to make a luscious Portuguese-inspired sauce. Ruby port provides the best color, but tawny port will also taste good.

PREP TIME 3 MINUTES   **COOK TIME** 45 MINUTES
SERVES 4

8	dried figs, tough stems removed
1	cup water
⅔	cup plus 1 tablespoon port
2	3-inch-long strips lemon zest
1	chicken (3 to 3 ½ pounds), quartered
1	tablespoon olive oil
	Salt
	Fresh-ground black pepper
1	tablespoon butter, cut into four pieces

1. Heat the oven to 375°. Pierce each fig three or four times with a paring knife. In a small stainless-steel saucepan, combine the figs, water, the ⅔ cup port, and the lemon zest. Bring to a boil and simmer, covered, until tender, about 30 minutes. Discard the zest and reserve the poaching liquid. Cut the figs in half.

2. Meanwhile, coat the chicken with the oil and arrange the pieces, skin-side up, in a large roasting pan. Sprinkle the chicken with the remaining 1 tablespoon port and season with ¼ teaspoon salt and ⅛ teaspoon pepper. Top each piece of chicken with a piece of the butter. Cook until the breasts are just done, about 30 minutes. Remove the breasts and continue to cook the legs until done, about 5 minutes longer. Remove the roasting pan from the oven; return the breasts to the pan.

3. Heat the broiler. Broil the chicken until the skin is golden brown, about 2 minutes. Transfer the chicken to a plate.

4. Pour off the fat from the roasting pan. Set the pan over moderate heat and add the fig-poaching liquid. Bring to a boil, scraping the bottom of the pan to dislodge any brown bits. Boil until reduced to approximately ¼ cup, about 4 minutes. Add the figs, any accumulated juices from the chicken, and a pinch each of salt and pepper. Spoon the sauce over the chicken.

MENU SUGGESTION
A green vegetable, such as steamed broccoli, makes a quick and easy side dish.

wine recommendation

A Portuguese red wine such as a Dão, combining soft texture with full flavor, is a geographical match. The savory sauce would also go nicely with a fruity cabernet sauvignon or merlot from either California or Australia.

spiced chicken breasts with dried apricots

A paste made of ground sesame seeds, almonds, cumin, coriander, and oregano gives both the chicken and the apricots delicious flavor.

PREP TIME 10 MINUTES   **COOK TIME** 30 MINUTES

SERVES 4

¾	cup dried apricots
1½	cups water
½	cup sliced almonds
⅓	cup sesame seeds
2	tablespoons ground cumin
2	tablespoons ground coriander
2	tablespoons paprika
2	tablespoons dried oregano
	Salt
¼	cup olive oil
2	tablespoons lemon juice
4	bone-in chicken breasts (about 2¼ pounds in all)

1. Heat the oven to 425°. In a small saucepan, combine the apricots and water. Bring to a boil, lower the heat, and then simmer, partially covered, for 10 minutes. Set aside.

2. Toast the almonds and sesame seeds in the oven until just beginning to brown, about 2 minutes. Transfer ⅓ cup of the almonds and ¼ cup of the sesame seeds to a blender; pulverize with the cumin, coriander, paprika, oregano, and ½ teaspoon salt. Put the mixture in a small bowl; stir in the oil and lemon juice to make a paste. Stir half of the paste into the apricots and water.

3. Put the chicken breasts in a small roasting pan, skin-side up, and coat with the remaining paste. Pour the apricot mixture around the chicken. Cook in the lower third of the oven until done, 20 to 25 minutes. If the chicken seems to be browning too quickly, cover the pan with aluminum foil the last 10 minutes of cooking.

4. Transfer the chicken to a plate. Spoon the fat from the pan. Serve the chicken topped with the apricots and any pan juices. Sprinkle the remaining almonds and sesame seeds over all.

MENU SUGGESTIONS

Steamed rice is an ideal accompaniment. So are roasted potatoes cooked alongside the chicken in a separate pan.

wine recommendation

A red or white wine with low tannin and plenty of fruit flavor will match the sweet, tangy apricots. For a red, a pinot noir from Oregon would be a good choice; for a white, a pinot blanc from Alsace in France.

orange-glazed chicken wings

Roll up your sleeves and dig into dinner! Orange juice and zest, soy sauce, and plenty of garlic coat these wings with fabulous flavor.

PREP TIME 10 MINUTES **COOK TIME** 30 MINUTES
SERVES 4

1   cup fresh orange juice (from about 2 oranges)
2   tablespoons grated orange zest
     (from about 3 oranges)
6   cloves garlic, minced
¼   cup soy sauce
1   tablespoon brown sugar
1½   teaspoons salt
½   teaspoon fresh-ground black pepper
4   pounds chicken wings

1. Heat the oven to 400°. In a large bowl, combine the orange juice with the orange zest, garlic, soy sauce, brown sugar, salt, and pepper. Add the chicken wings and toss to coat.

2. On two large baking sheets, arrange the wings in a single layer. Reserve ¼ cup of the orange mixture and spoon the rest of the mixture over the wings. Bake for 20 minutes. Turn the wings over and baste them with the reserved orange mixture. Cook until just done, about 10 minutes longer.

MENU SUGGESTIONS
Serve this finger food with a vegetable that you can also eat with your hands, such as strips of raw fennel or jicama.

TEST-KITCHEN TIP
When you grate the orange zest, remove only the orange layer of the skin, leaving the bitter white pith behind.

wine recommendation
Sweet, salty, and spicy, this dish really needs a wine with good acidity, moderate alcohol, and just a touch of sweetness. Look for a low-alcohol German kabinett riesling or a semi-dry riesling from the Finger Lakes region of New York.

jerk chicken

Jamaicans love this sweet-and-spicy rub on both chicken and meat. Our rub is a little less fiery than the traditional version, but if you'd like to kick the heat up a notch, just add more cayenne pepper.

PREP TIME 5 MINUTES   **COOK TIME** 30 MINUTES
MARINATING TIME: 30 MINUTES
SERVES 4

3	scallions including green tops, chopped
2	cloves garlic, chopped
1	tablespoon ground allspice
1	tablespoon dried thyme
1	teaspoon cayenne
½	teaspoon fresh-ground black pepper
1¼	teaspoons salt
1	teaspoon grated nutmeg
2	tablespoons brown sugar
¼	teaspoon vinegar
¼	cup cooking oil
4	whole chicken legs

1. In a food processor or blender, puree all the ingredients except the chicken legs. Put the chicken in a large roasting pan and coat with the pureed mixture. Let the chicken marinate for about 30 minutes.

2. Heat the oven to 450°. Cook the chicken legs in the upper third of the oven for 15 minutes. Turn the legs over and cook until just done, about 15 minutes longer.

MENU SUGGESTIONS

Corn bread, rice and beans (or just plain rice), or corn on the cob would all taste great with this highly spiced chicken. Fried plantains are another authentic accompaniment.

TEST-KITCHEN TIP

The longer you can marinate the chicken legs, the more the flavor will penetrate the meat. We've suggested 30 minutes, but you can marinate the chicken for up to 24 hours.

wine recommendation

The strong flavors in this recipe will be best with a refreshing wine that combines low alcohol and good acidity. Try a slightly chilled Beaujolais from France. Or open a cold bottle of light-bodied beer.

baked buffalo chicken wings

Most of us think of Buffalo wings as bar food, but with their accompaniment of celery sticks and creamy blue-cheese dressing, they make a fine casual meal. These wings are hot, but if you like them incendiary, pass extra Tabasco at the table.

PREP TIME 10 MINUTES   **COOK TIME** 25 MINUTES

SERVES 4

4	pounds chicken wings
3	tablespoons cooking oil
4	cloves garlic, chopped
1¾	teaspoons salt
1½	teaspoons cayenne
⅔	cup mayonnaise
⅓	cup sour cream
¼	pound blue cheese, crumbled (about 1 cup)
2	scallions including green tops, chopped
5	teaspoons vinegar
¼	teaspoon fresh-ground black pepper
¼	cup ketchup
1	tablespoon Tabasco sauce
8	ribs celery, cut into sticks

1. Heat the oven to 425°. In a large bowl, combine the wings, oil, garlic, 1½ teaspoons of the salt, and the cayenne. Arrange the wings in a single layer on two large baking sheets. Bake until just done, about 25 minutes.

2. Meanwhile, in a medium glass or stainless-steel bowl, combine the mayonnaise, sour cream, blue cheese, scallions, 1 teaspoon of the vinegar, the remaining ¼ teaspoon salt, and the black pepper.

3. In a large bowl, combine the ketchup, the remaining 4 teaspoons vinegar, and the Tabasco sauce. Add the wings and toss to coat. Serve the wings with the celery sticks and blue-cheese dressing alongside.

MENU SUGGESTIONS

Pair these wings with more finger food. Corn on the cob would go nicely. Roasted potato wedges are a good alternative and can be cooked alongside the wings.

wine recommendation

Beer is a no-brainer with the salt, spice, and heat of this barfly classic. For a more festive alternative, serve a crisp sparkling wine; it will refresh the palate and tame the heat of the dish.

chicken with lemon, oregano, & feta cheese

A trio of Greek flavors gives these chicken quarters Mediterranean flair. The cheese is sprinkled over the cooked chicken, which is then broiled until golden.

PREP TIME 3 MINUTES   **COOK TIME** 40 MINUTES
SERVES 4

1	chicken (3 to 3½ pounds), quartered
1	tablespoon olive oil
1½	teaspoons dried oregano
1	tablespoon lemon juice
¼	teaspoon salt
⅛	teaspoon fresh-ground black pepper
1	tablespoon butter, cut into 4 pieces
1½	ounces feta cheese, crumbled (about ⅓ cup)

1. Heat the oven to 375°. Coat the chicken with the oil; arrange the pieces, skin-side up, in a large roasting pan. Sprinkle the chicken with the oregano, lemon juice, salt, and pepper. Top each piece of chicken with a piece of the butter.

2. Cook the chicken until the breasts are just done, about 30 minutes. Remove the breasts and continue to cook the legs until done, about 5 minutes longer. Remove the roasting pan from the oven; return the breasts to the pan. Top the chicken pieces with the feta cheese. Press any cheese that rolls off into the pan back onto the chicken. Baste the chicken with the pan juices.

3. Heat the broiler. Broil the chicken until the cheese is melted and golden brown, about 2 minutes. Serve with the pan juices.

MENU SUGGESTIONS
Balance the tanginess of lemon and feta with a mild side dish such as sautéed zucchini or orzo tossed with a little olive oil.

wine recommendation

This Greek-flavored dish will go nicely with a number of rustic, spicy red wines. Try finding a bottle from the Greek island of Paros or Santorini. Another alternative would be a syrah-based wine such as a Crozes-Hermitage from the northern Rhône Valley in France.

chicken breasts with creamy vegetable topping

Red bell pepper, scallion, and carrot are sautéed briefly, then mixed with cream cheese to form a bright, speckled sauce that bakes right on the chicken—simple and delicious.

PREP TIME 7 MINUTES   **COOK TIME** 30 MINUTES
SERVES 4

1	tablespoon cooking oil
1	red bell pepper, chopped
2	scallions including green tops, chopped
1	carrot, grated
8	ounces cream cheese, at room temperature
1	teaspoon salt
½	teaspoon fresh-ground black pepper
4	bone-in chicken breasts (about 2 ¼ pounds in all), skin removed

1. Heat the oven to 425°. In a medium frying pan, heat the oil over moderate heat. Add the bell pepper and cook, stirring occasionally, until starting to soften, about 3 minutes. Add the scallions and carrot and cook 2 minutes longer. Mix the vegetables with the cream cheese, ¾ teaspoon of the salt, and ¼ teaspoon of the black pepper.

2. Sprinkle the chicken breasts with the remaining ¼ teaspoons of salt and pepper. Put the breasts in a roasting pan and spread them with the vegetable cream cheese. Bake the chicken until just done, 20 to 25 minutes.

MENU SUGGESTIONS

The rich topping on the chicken leaves one wanting a simply-prepared vegetable, such as steamed asparagus, broccoli, or green beans.

VARIATION

Chicken Breasts with Boursin-Cheese Sauce
Substitute a 5 ½-ounce package of plain or garlic-and-herb-flavored Boursin cheese for the cream cheese.

wine recommendation

A crisp and fruity white will cut through the rich cheese and pair well with the acidity of the bell pepper and scallion. A kabinett riesling from the Mosel-Saar-Ruwer region of Germany or, if you can find it, a riesling from the Finger Lakes in New York is a good possibility.

chicken & eggplant parmesan

In this delicious new take on classic eggplant Parmesan, broiled eggplant is layered with fresh mozzarella, basil, and slices of chicken. If basil isn't in season, don't turn to dried basil; it has little flavor. Substitute 1 teaspoon dried marjoram instead, adding it to the tomato sauce with the salt.

PREP TIME 6 MINUTES   **COOK TIME** 30 MINUTES

REST TIME 5 MINUTES

SERVES 4

1	small eggplant (about 1 pound), cut into ¼-inch rounds
4	tablespoons olive oil
1	teaspoon salt
	Fresh-ground black pepper
1	pound boneless, skinless chicken breasts (about 3)
2	cups canned crushed tomatoes in thick puree
½	pound fresh mozzarella, cut into thin slices
⅓	cup grated Parmesan cheese
¼	cup lightly packed basil leaves

1. Heat the broiler. Arrange the eggplant in a single layer on a large baking sheet. Coat both sides of the eggplant with 2½ tablespoons of the oil and sprinkle with ½ teaspoon of the salt and ¼ teaspoon pepper. Broil, turning once, until browned, about 5 minutes per side. Turn off the broiler and heat the oven to 425°.

2. In a large nonstick frying pan, heat 1 tablespoon of the oil over moderately high heat. Season the chicken with ¼ teaspoon of the salt and ⅛ teaspoon pepper and add to the pan. Partially cook the chicken for 2 minutes per side and remove from the pan. When cool enough to handle, cut the chicken crosswise into ¼-inch slices.

3. Oil an 8-inch square baking dish. Put one third of the eggplant in a single layer in the dish. Top with half of the chicken, half of the tomatoes, half of the mozzarella, one third of the Parmesan, half of the basil, and the remaining ¼ teaspoon of salt. Repeat with another third of the eggplant, the remaining chicken, tomatoes, and mozzarella, another third of the Parmesan, and the remaining basil. Top with the remaining eggplant and sprinkle with the remaining cheese. Drizzle with the remaining ½ tablespoon oil. Bake for 20 minutes and let sit for 5 minutes before cutting.

wine recommendation

An Italian red wine such as a reasonably-priced nebbiolo from either the Piedmont or Lombardy region has plenty of acidity and enough body to stand up to the rich taste of this dish.

chicken & brussels sprouts over white-bean & rosemary puree

A drizzle of pan juices ties everything together to make a complete meal that's welcome during the winter. Cannellini, one of our favorite canned beans, make a quick, delicious puree.

PREP TIME 5 MINUTES   **COOK TIME** 40 MINUTES
SERVES 4

- ¾   pound Brussels sprouts, cut in half from top to stem
- 4   tablespoons olive oil
    Salt
    Fresh-ground black pepper
- 4   chicken thighs
- 4   chicken drumsticks
- 2   cloves garlic, minced
- 1   teaspoon dried rosemary, crumbled, or 1 tablespoon chopped fresh rosemary
- 4   cups drained and rinsed white beans, preferably cannellini (from two 19-ounce cans)
- ½   cup water
- 2   tablespoons chopped flat-leaf parsley

1. Heat the oven to 450°. In a medium bowl, toss the Brussels sprouts with 1 tablespoon of the oil, ¼ teaspoon of salt, and ¼ of teaspoon pepper. Set aside.

2. Put the chicken pieces in a large roasting pan and toss with 1 tablespoon of oil, ¼ teaspoon salt, and ¼ teaspoon pepper. Arrange the chicken pieces about 1 inch apart, skin-side up, and roast for 25 minutes. Add the Brussels sprouts and continue cooking until the chicken and sprouts are done, about 12 minutes longer. Transfer them to a plate and leave to rest in a warm spot for about 5 minutes.

3. Meanwhile, in a medium saucepan, heat the remaining 2 tablespoons oil, the garlic, and the rosemary over low heat, stirring, for 3 minutes. Raise the heat to moderate and add the beans, ¼ cup of the water, ¼ teaspoon salt, and ⅛ teaspoon pepper. Cook, mashing the beans to a coarse puree, until hot, about 5 minutes. Stir in the parsley.

4. Pour off the fat from the roasting pan. Set the pan over moderate heat and add the remaining ¼ cup water. Bring to a boil, scraping the bottom of the pan to dislodge any brown bits. Boil until reduced to ¼ cup, about 4 minutes. Add any accumulated juices from the chicken and a pinch each of salt and pepper. Spoon the white-bean puree onto plates and top with the chicken, the Brussels sprouts, and then the pan juices.

wine recommendation

Pair this Mediterranean-inspired dish with a full-flavored red from France. Try one from the southern Rhône Valley such as a Châteauneuf-du-Pape or a Côtes-du-Rhône.

cornish hens with scallion butter & lime

The typical Mexican combination of cumin and lime works beautifully with Cornish hens. Scallion butter both moistens the hens and adds an extra fillip of flavor.

PREP TIME 5 MINUTES   **COOK TIME** 20 MINUTES
SERVES 4

4   tablespoons butter, at room temperature
1   teaspoon dried oregano
1   teaspoon cumin
½   teaspoon salt
     Fresh-ground black pepper
2   Cornish hens (about 1¼ pounds each), halved
1   scallion including green top, chopped
     Lime wedges, for serving

1. Heat the oven to 450°. In a small bowl, combine 2 tablespoons of the butter with the oregano, cumin, ¼ teaspoon of the salt, and ¼ teaspoon pepper.
2. Rub the mixture over the skin of the hens and arrange them, skin-side up, on a baking sheet. Roast in the upper third of the oven until golden and cooked through, about 20 minutes.

3. Meanwhile, combine the remaining 2 tablespoons butter with the scallion, the remaining ¼ teaspoon salt, and ⅛ teaspoon pepper. When the hens are roasted, top with the scallion butter. Serve with lime wedges.

MENU SUGGESTIONS
You could roast new potatoes right alongside the hens with almost no effort. Sautéed bell peppers would complete the meal.

VARIATION
Cornish Hens with Herb Butter & Lime
Mix 1 tablespoon chopped fresh herbs, such as chives, parsley, and/or oregano, with the butter in place of the scallions.

wine recommendation

A number of hearty red wines would be nice with the straightforward, rustic flavors here. Look for a Corbières from the south of France, a zinfandel from California, or a Rosso di Montalcino from Tuscany in Italy.

cornish hens with fruit, walnuts, & honey-apple glaze

Dried fruits, fresh apples, and nuts make a delightful dressing for these roasted Cornish hens. The dish seems perfect for a chilly fall evening, but it can certainly be served any time of the year.

PREP TIME 10 MINUTES   **COOK TIME** 25 MINUTES

SERVES 4

2	tart apples, such as Granny Smith, peeled, cored, and diced
⅔	cup dried apricots, cut into thin slices
⅔	cup raisins
1	cup walnuts, chopped
¼	teaspoon cinnamon
2	tablespoons melted butter
¼	cup apple juice
2	tablespoons honey
¼	teaspoon dried thyme
½	teaspoon salt
2	Cornish hens (about 1¼ pounds each), halved
¼	teaspoon fresh-ground black pepper

1. Heat the oven to 425°. In a roasting pan, combine the apples, apricots, raisins, walnuts, cinnamon, and butter. Spread the mixture over the bottom of the pan.

2. In a small bowl, combine the apple juice, honey, thyme, and ¼ teaspoon of the salt to make a glaze. Sprinkle the Cornish hens with the remaining ¼ teaspoon salt and the pepper and set them breast-side down on top of the fruit-and-nut mixture. Brush the hens with some of the glaze and then cook for 10 minutes.

3. Remove the roasting pan from the oven. Stir the fruit-and-nut mixture and turn the hens over. Brush them with more of the glaze, return the pan to the oven, and cook until just done, about 15 minutes longer. Glaze the hens one final time and serve them with the fruit-and-nut dressing.

MENU SUGGESTIONS

Earthy wild rice or bulgar pilaf will balance the sweet fruit glaze here.

wine recommendation

The fruits and nuts in this dish will pair well with the rich texture and flavor of a Tokay Pinot Gris, a white from Alsace in France. A red wine with plenty of fruit flavor, such as a grenache from California, would be another good match.

grilled chicken breasts with grapefruit glaze

Simply prepared yet special, these chicken breasts are grilled and basted with a bitter, tart, and sweet glaze.

PREP TIME 5 MINUTES   **COOK TIME** 20 MINUTES
SERVES 4

2	cloves garlic, minced
1	teaspoon grapefruit zest (from about ½ grapefruit)
½	cup grapefruit juice (from 1 grapefruit)
1	tablespoon cooking oil
2	tablespoons honey
½	teaspoon salt
¼	teaspoon fresh-ground black pepper
4	bone-in chicken breasts (about 2¼ pounds in all)

1. Light the grill. In a small bowl, combine the garlic, grapefruit zest, grapefruit juice, oil, honey, salt, and pepper.

2. Grill the chicken breasts over moderately high heat, brushing frequently with the glaze, for 8 minutes. Turn and cook, brushing with more glaze, until the chicken is just done, 10 to 12 minutes longer. Remove.

3. In a small stainless-steel saucepan, bring the remaining glaze to a boil. Boil for about 1 minute, remove from the heat, and pour over the grilled chicken.

MENU SUGGESTIONS

Since the chicken breasts don't have a lot of sauce, serve a juicy vegetable such as grilled or sautéed summer squash or zucchini alongside.

VARIATION

Grilled Chicken Breasts with Citrus Glaze

Use a combination of citrus juices, such as orange, lemon, or lime, instead of all or part of the grapefruit juice.

wine recommendation

The crisp acidity, effervescence, and moderate alcohol level of a brut Champagne from France or a sparkling wine from California will be perfect with the smoky taste of the chicken and with the high acidity of the grapefruit juice.

grilled chicken with spicy brazilian tomato & coconut sauce

Redolent of ginger and jalapeños, the tomato sauce is a lively addition to plain grilled chicken. If you like less heat, use only one jalapeño.

PREP TIME 6 MINUTES   **COOK TIME** 20 TO 26 MINUTES

SERVES 4

4	tablespoons cooking oil
3	cloves garlic, minced
1	chicken (3 to 3½ pounds), quartered
¾	teaspoon salt
	Fresh-ground black pepper
1	onion, chopped
1	tablespoon minced fresh ginger
2	jalapeño peppers, seeds and ribs removed, minced
1¼	cups canned crushed tomatoes in thick puree
1	cup canned unsweetened coconut milk
2	tablespoons chopped cilantro or parsley

1. Light the grill. In a shallow dish, combine 3 tablespoons of the oil with two-thirds of the minced garlic. Coat the chicken with half of the garlic oil and season with ¼ teaspoon of the salt and ⅛ teaspoon pepper. Grill the chicken over moderately high heat, basting with the remaining garlic oil, until just done, about 10 minutes per side for the breasts, 13 for the legs.

2. Meanwhile, in a medium saucepan, heat the remaining 1 tablespoon oil over moderately low heat. Add the onion and cook, stirring occasionally, until translucent, about 5 minutes. Add the remaining garlic, the ginger, and the jalapeños, and cook, stirring, for 1 minute longer. Add the tomatoes, the coconut milk, the remaining ½ teaspoon salt, and a pinch of pepper. Bring to a simmer and cook, stirring occasionally, until thickened, about 5 minutes. Stir in the cilantro and serve with the chicken.

MENU SUGGESTIONS

Rice and beans or refried beans are typical Brazilian side dishes that taste especially good with chicken, as well as a crisp salad.

wine recommendation

This spicy dish will demolish any subtlety in a wine. Go for something straightforward and gulpable: a fresh white wine such as a pinot bianco from northern Italy, a slightly chilled red such as Beaujolais from France, or a beer.

grilled tandoori chicken

Flavored by a yogurt and spice paste with ginger, cumin, and coriander, this chicken tastes almost as good as if it were cooked in a tandoor oven. Like Indian cooks, we remove the chicken skin and score the flesh so that the spice paste penetrates.

PREP TIME 5 MINUTES **MARINATING TIME** 15 MINUTES
COOK TIME 20 TO 24 MINUTES
SERVES 4

1	chicken (3 to 3½ pounds), cut into 8 pieces and skin removed
3	tablespoons lemon juice
1½	tablespoons water
1½	teaspoons salt
¼	teaspoon ground turmeric
½	cup plain yogurt
2	large garlic cloves, chopped
1	tablespoon chopped fresh ginger
1¼	teaspoons ground coriander
¾	teaspoon ground cumin
⅛	teaspoon cayenne
3	tablespoons cooking oil

1. Light the grill. Using a sharp knife, cut shallow incisions in the chicken pieces at about ½-inch intervals. In a large, glass dish or stainless-steel pan, combine the lemon juice, water, salt, and turmeric. Add the chicken pieces and turn to coat. Let the chicken pieces marinate for 5 minutes.

2. Meanwhile, in a small bowl, combine the yogurt, garlic, ginger, coriander, cumin, and cayenne. Add to the chicken and lemon mixture; turn to coat. Let marinate for 10 minutes.

3. Grill the chicken over moderately high heat, basting with oil, for 10 minutes. Turn and cook, basting with the remaining oil, until just done, about 10 minutes longer for the breasts, 12 for the thighs and drumsticks.

MENU SUGGESTIONS

Indian flatbreads, such as naan, are the traditional accompaniment to tandoori. You can grill store-bought naan or other flatbread, such as pita or lavash. In summer, the sweetness of grilled corn on the cob makes a nice balance to the spiciness of the chicken. Another option is eggplant, a favorite vegetable in India, sliced and grilled.

wine recommendation

Spicy dishes such as this pair best with wines with low alcohol, high acidity, and a touch of fruitiness. Try an off-dry riesling from Oregon, California, or New York State.

grilled cornish hens with sun-dried tomato pesto

Since the tomato pesto here is made in a processor or blender, you have to make more than the small quantity needed. Use leftover pesto later in the week on grilled vegetables or fish. It's also a delicious addition to sandwiches, not to mention pasta.

PREP TIME 7 MINUTES   **COOK TIME** 24 MINUTES
SERVES 4

- ⅔ cup reconstituted sun-dried tomatoes, or sun-dried tomatoes packed in oil, drained
- 2 cloves garlic, chopped
- 3 tablespoons grated Parmesan cheese
- ¾ teaspoon salt
- ¼ teaspoon fresh-ground black pepper
- 1 tablespoon lemon juice
- ½ cup olive oil
- 2 Cornish hens (about 1¼ pounds each), halved

1. Light the grill. In a food processor or blender, mince the tomatoes and garlic with the Parmesan, salt, pepper, and lemon juice. With the machine running, add the oil in a thin stream and continue whirring until the ingredients are well mixed.

2. With your fingers, loosen the skin from the breast meat of each hen, leaving the skin around the edge attached. For each half hen, spread 1 tablespoon of pesto under the skin and 1 tablespoon over it.

3. Grill the hens over moderate heat, skin-side down, for 12 minutes. Turn the hens and cook until just done, about 12 minutes longer.

MENU SUGGESTIONS

Creamy polenta topped with a dollop of the extra pesto will be perfect with the hens. Also, since the grill is already hot, you might want to throw on some vegetables—such as peppers, zucchini, or asparagus.

RECONSTITUTING SUN-DRIED TOMATOES

In a small pan, bring enough water to a boil to cover the dried tomatoes. Add the tomatoes, then remove from the heat and let them steep in the hot water for about 5 minutes. Drain.

wine recommendation

For this grilled dish, with its smoke, salt, and acidity (from tomatoes), a wine that's simple and refreshing is the best choice. Among the many options are Italian red wines with good acidity such as Chianti Classico or dolcetto.

grilled cornish hens with rice & sicilian butter

The traditional combination of olives, anchovies, and oranges shows up here in a flavored butter that adds a special richness and intensity to hens hot off the grill. Make a double batch and keep the extra in your freezer to use at a moment's notice.

PREP TIME 6 MINUTES   **COOK TIME** 24 MINUTES
SERVES 4

8	tablespoons butter, at room temperature
⅓	cup black olives, such as Kalamata, halved and pitted
2	teaspoons anchovy paste
1	tablespoon grated orange zest (from about 1 navel orange)
2	teaspoons orange juice
2	cloves garlic, minced
¼	teaspoon fresh-ground black pepper
2	Cornish hens (about 1 ¼ pounds each), halved
2	tablespoons cooking oil
	Boiled or steamed rice, for serving

1. Light the grill. In a food processor, puree the butter and olives with the anchovy paste, orange zest, orange juice, garlic, and pepper. With a rubber spatula, scrape the butter into a small bowl and refrigerate.

2. Rub the hens with oil and grill over moderate heat for 12 minutes. Turn and cook until just done, about 12 minutes longer.

3. Remove the hens from the grill and serve with the rice. Top each serving with 2 tablespoons of the flavored butter, letting the butter melt over both the hen and the rice.

MENU SUGGESTIONS

You might grill some eggplant slices and drizzle them with balsamic vinegar to go with these hens. Sautéed broccoli rabe with garlic and a sprinkling of Parmesan would also match the Italian mood.

wine recommendation

The saltiness of olives and anchovies can make the wrong wine appear coarse and too alcoholic. A rosé is the perfect choice. If you can find one from Sicily, buy it. If not, pick a bottle from Navarre in Spain or from the south of France.

grilled asian cornish hens with asparagus & portobello mushrooms

Though marinated only briefly with lime juice, garlic, ginger, and soy sauce, the Cornish hens and vegetables nevertheless have a deliciously intense flavor.

PREP TIME 5 MINUTES   **COOK TIME** 24 MINUTES
MARINATING TIME 10 MINUTES
SERVES 4

6   tablespoons soy sauce

¼   cup lime juice (from about 2 limes)

¼   cup cooking oil

4   cloves garlic, minced

1   teaspoon ground ginger

½   teaspoon fresh-ground black pepper

¼   teaspoon salt

2   Cornish hens (about 1¼ pounds each), halved

1   pound asparagus

⅔   pound portobello mushrooms, stems removed, caps cut into 1/4-inch slices, or 6 ounces sliced portobello mushrooms

1. Light the grill. In a small glass or stainless-steel bowl, combine the soy sauce, lime juice, oil, garlic, ginger, pepper, and salt. Put the hens into two large glass dishes. Pour ½ cup of the marinade over them and turn to coat. Let marinate, turning once, for 10 minutes.

2. Grill the hens over moderate heat for 12 minutes. Turn and cook until just done, about 12 minutes longer.

3. Meanwhile, snap off and discard the tough ends of the asparagus. In a medium bowl, toss the asparagus spears with 2 tablespoons of the remaining marinade and grill for about 12 minutes, turning once.

4. In the same bowl, toss the mushrooms with the remaining 2 tablespoons marinade and grill for about 5 minutes per side. Serve the hens with the asparagus and mushrooms alongside.

MENU SUGGESTIONS
Make your whole dinner outdoors by adding new potatoes or sweet-potato wedges to the grill.

wine recommendation

An acidic, assertively flavored white wine, such as a sauvignon blanc from Australia or South Africa, is great with the asparagus and the bold flavors of the soy sauce and lime juice.

Chicken Provençal
on page 134.

5

sautés &
stir-fries

pecan-crusted chicken with mustard sauce

Nutty sautéed chicken dipped in a creamy mustard sauce delivers nicely varied textures and flavors. Using cornstarch rather than flour makes the crust especially crisp.

PREP TIME 10 MINUTES **COOK TIME** 10–11 MINUTES
SERVES 4

1   cup pecans
2   tablespoons cornstarch
1   teaspoon dried thyme
1   teaspoon paprika
1½   teaspoons salt
     Cayenne
1   egg
2   tablespoons water
4   boneless, skinless chicken breasts
     (about 1⅓ pounds in all)
3   tablespoons cooking oil
1   cup mayonnaise
2   tablespoons grainy or Dijon mustard
½   teaspoon white-wine vinegar
½   teaspoon sugar
2   tablespoons chopped fresh parsley

1. In a food processor, pulse the pecans with the cornstarch, thyme, paprika, 1¼ teaspoons of the salt, and ⅛ teaspoon cayenne until the nuts are chopped fine. Transfer the mixture to a medium bowl.

2. Whisk together the egg and the water in a small bowl. Dip each chicken breast into the egg mixture and then into the nut mixture.

3. In a large nonstick frying pan, heat the oil over moderate heat. Add the chicken to the pan and cook for 5 minutes. Turn and continue cooking until the chicken is golden brown and cooked through, 5 to 6 minutes longer.

4. Meanwhile, in a small bowl, combine the mayonnaise, mustard, vinegar, sugar, parsley, a pinch of cayenne, and the remaining ¼ teaspoon salt. Serve the chicken with the mustard dipping sauce.

MENU SUGGESTIONS

The crisp coating on the chicken invites a creamy potato gratin alongside. Green beans, perhaps sautéed in bacon fat, would taste great, too.

wine recommendation

The combination of the sweet pecans and the assertive mustard sauce lends itself to either a crisp sparkling wine or a stainless-steel–fermented sauvignon blanc from California.

sautéed chicken breasts with fennel & rosemary

The Mediterranean flavors of fennel, garlic, and rosemary are perfect with chicken. The fennel and chicken are sautéed and then briefly braised in chicken broth, which becomes a tasty light sauce.

PREP TIME 7 MINUTES   **COOK TIME** 23 MINUTES

REST TIME 5 MINUTES

SERVES 4

2	tablespoons olive oil
1	large fennel bulb (about 1¼ pounds), cut into ½-inch slices
2	teaspoons dried rosemary, crumbled
½	teaspoon salt
½	cup canned low-sodium chicken broth or homemade stock
4	boneless, skinless chicken breasts (about 1⅓ pounds in all)
¼	teaspoon fresh-ground black pepper
2	cloves garlic, minced
2	tablespoons chopped flat-leaf parsley

1. In a large nonstick frying pan, heat 1 tablespoon of the oil over moderately high heat. Add the fennel, 1 teaspoon of the rosemary, and ¼ teaspoon of the salt. Cook, stirring frequently, until the fennel is golden brown and almost done, about 12 minutes. Add the broth and bring to a boil. Cover, reduce the heat and simmer until the fennel is tender, about 3 minutes. Remove the fennel and the cooking liquid from the pan.

2. Wipe out the pan and heat the remaining 1 tablespoon oil over moderate heat. Season the chicken with the remaining ¼ teaspoon salt and ⅛ teaspoon of the pepper. Add the chicken to the pan with the remaining 1 teaspoon of rosemary and cook until brown, about 5 minutes. Turn and cook until almost done, about 3 minutes longer. Add the garlic; cook, stirring, for 30 seconds. Add the fennel and its cooking liquid and the remaining ⅛ teaspoon pepper. Bring to a simmer. Cover the pan and remove from the heat. Let steam 5 minutes. Stir in the parsley.

MENU SUGGESTIONS

Soft polenta is an appropriate accompaniment to this Italian-style dish. Mashed potatoes are another good match.

wine recommendation

The fennel and the rosemary will pair especially nicely with a full-bodied red wine that has a hint of sweetness, such as a Rioja from Spain.

chicken chasseur

A French classic that never seems to go out of style, this dish combines mushrooms and chicken in a tomato and white-wine sauce. The name, literally "hunter's chicken," harks back to a time when game birds and mushrooms from the woods were a natural autumn combination.

PREP TIME 6 MINUTES   **COOK TIME** 30 MINUTES
SERVES 4

1	tablespoon cooking oil
4	bone-in chicken breasts (about 2¼ pounds in all)
1	teaspoon salt
½	teaspoon fresh-ground black pepper
1	tablespoon butter
1	onion, chopped
¾	pound mushrooms, sliced
2	cloves garlic, minced
1½	teaspoons flour
6	tablespoons dry vermouth or dry white wine
⅔	cup canned low-sodium chicken broth or homemade stock
1	cup canned crushed tomatoes, drained
¼	teaspoon dried thyme
2	tablespoons chopped fresh parsley

1. In a large, deep frying pan, heat the oil over moderately high heat. Season the chicken with ¼ teaspoon each of the salt and pepper and add to the pan. Cook until browned, turning, about 8 minutes in all. Remove. Pour off all but 1 tablespoon fat from the pan.

2. Add the butter to the pan and reduce the heat to moderately low. Add the onion and cook, stirring occasionally, until translucent, about 5 minutes. Raise the heat to moderately high. Add the mushrooms, garlic, and ¼ teaspoon of the salt. Cook, stirring frequently, until the vegetables are browned, about 5 minutes.

3. Add the flour and cook, stirring, for 30 seconds. Stir in the vermouth and bring back to a simmer. Stir in the broth, tomatoes, thyme, and the remaining ½ teaspoon salt. Add the chicken and any accumulated juices. Reduce the heat; simmer, covered, until the chicken is done, about 10 minutes. Stir in the parsley and the remaining ¼ teaspoon pepper.

wine recommendation

This earthy dish is perfectly suited to the rustic charms of a country red wine from southwestern France. Look for a bottle from one of the various appellations in that region, such as Cahors, Madiran, or Bergerac.

kung pao chicken

Quick Asian stir-fries make especially satisfying weeknight dinners. Kung pao is traditionally a seriously spicy dish, but we've given ours a moderate level of heat; feel free to adjust the quantity of red-pepper flakes to suit your taste. Serve with steamed rice.

PREP TIME 10 MINUTES   **COOK TIME** 5–6 MINUTES
SERVES 4

- 1⅓ pounds boneless, skinless chicken breasts (about 4), cut into ½-inch pieces
- 5 tablespoons soy sauce
- 2 tablespoons sherry
- 1 tablespoon plus 2 teaspoons cornstarch
- 2 teaspoons sugar
- 2 tablespoons white-wine vinegar or rice vinegar
- 2 teaspoons Asian sesame oil
- ⅓ cup water
- 2 tablespoons cooking oil
- ½ cup peanuts
- 4 scallions, white bulbs and green tops cut separately into ½-inch pieces
- ¼ teaspoon dried red-pepper flakes

1. In a medium bowl, toss the chicken with 1 tablespoon of the soy sauce, 1 tablespoon of the sherry, and the 1 tablespoon cornstarch.

2. In a small bowl, combine the sugar, vinegar, sesame oil, water, and the remaining 4 tablespoons of soy sauce, 1 tablespoon of sherry, and 2 teaspoons cornstarch.

3. In a wok or large frying pan, heat 1 tablespoon of the oil over moderately high heat. Add the peanuts and stir-fry until light brown, about 30 seconds. Remove from the pan. Heat the remaining 1 tablespoon oil. Add the white part of the scallions and the red-pepper flakes to the pan and cook, stirring, for 30 seconds. Add the chicken with its marinade and cook, stirring, until almost done, 1 to 2 minutes. Add the soy-sauce mixture and the scallion tops and simmer until the chicken is just done, about 1 minute longer. Stir in the peanuts.

VARIATION

Cashew Chicken
Substitute the same amount of cashews for the peanuts.

wine recommendation

Since the chicken is salty and spicy, the drink's first job is to refresh. An aromatic white wine such as a sauvignon blanc from California or South Africa will do nicely, as will your favorite cold beer.

stir-fried chicken with chinese cabbage

A simple sauce of garlic, hot pepper, sherry, wine vinegar, and tomato adds intense flavor to this quick stir-fry, and it practically makes itself while the chicken and cabbage cook. Steamed rice is an ideal accompaniment.

PREP TIME 10 MINUTES   **COOK TIME** 10–12 MINUTES
MARINATING TIME 10 MINUTES
SERVES 4

1⅓ pounds boneless, skinless chicken breasts
    (about 4), cut into 1-inch pieces
1   tablespoon plus 4 teaspoons soy sauce
3   tablespoons dry sherry
¼   teaspoon cayenne
2   tablespoons cooking oil
1   onion, chopped
2   cloves garlic, minced
1   teaspoon ground coriander
1   tablespoon wine vinegar
½   head Chinese cabbage (about 1 pound), sliced
¾   cup drained sliced water chestnuts
    (from one 8-ounce can)
2   teaspoons tomato paste
¼   teaspoon dried red-pepper flakes
3   tablespoons water
3   tablespoons chopped cilantro or scallion tops
⅛   teaspoon salt

1. In a medium bowl, combine the chicken with the 1 tablespoon soy sauce, 1 tablespoon of the sherry, and the cayenne. Let marinate for 10 minutes.

2. In a wok or large frying pan, heat 1 tablespoon of the oil over moderately high heat. Add the chicken and cook, stirring, until almost done, 1 to 2 minutes. Remove.

3. Add the remaining 1 tablespoon oil to the pan. Add the onion, garlic, and coriander. Cook, stirring, until the onion is golden, about 4 minutes. Add the remaining 2 tablespoons sherry and the vinegar. Cook, stirring, 1 minute longer.

4. Add the cabbage, water chestnuts, the remaining 4 teaspoons soy sauce, the tomato paste, red-pepper flakes, and water and cook, stirring, for 3 minutes longer. Add the chicken and any accumulated juices, the cilantro, and the salt and cook, stirring, until the chicken is just done, 1 to 2 minutes longer.

wine recommendation

You need a straightforward white wine with plenty of acidity to survive the garlic, soy sauce, and hot pepper in this dish. A chenin blanc from the Loire Valley in France, particularly from Vouvray, Saumur, or Anjou, will be able to hold its own.

chicken provençal

The flavors are bold in this French sauté with a sauce of tomatoes, garlic, rosemary, olives, and just enough anchovy paste to give the sauce depth.

PREP TIME 8 MINUTES   **COOK TIME** 30–35 MINUTES
SERVES 4

1	tablespoon cooking oil
1	chicken (about 3 to 3½ pounds), cut into eight pieces
¾	teaspoon salt
½	teaspoon fresh-ground black pepper
1	small onion, chopped
4	cloves garlic, minced
½	cup red wine
1½	cups canned crushed tomatoes with their juice
½	teaspoon dried rosemary
½	teaspoon dried thyme
⅓	cup black olives, such as Niçoise or Kalamata, halved and pitted
1	teaspoon anchovy paste

1. In a large, deep frying pan, heat the oil over moderately high heat. Season the chicken with ¼ teaspoon each of the salt and pepper and put it in the pan. Cook the chicken until browned, turning, about 8 minutes in all. Remove the chicken from the pan. Pour off all but 1 tablespoon fat from the pan.

2. Reduce the heat to moderately low. Add the onion and the garlic and cook, stirring occasionally, until the onion starts to soften, about 3 minutes. Add the wine to the pan and simmer until reduced to about ¼ cup, 1 to 2 minutes. Add the tomatoes, rosemary, thyme, olives, anchovy paste, and the remaining ½ teaspoon salt and simmer for 5 minutes.

3. Add the chicken thighs and drumsticks and any accumulated juices. Reduce the heat to low and simmer, covered, for 10 minutes. Add the breasts and cook until the chicken is just done, about 10 minutes more. Add the remaining ¼ teaspoon pepper.

MENU SUGGESTIONS
Simple roasted new potatoes or steamed green beans would be excellent with the gutsy flavors here.

wine recommendation

There are lots of interesting wines from the region of Provence that will be ideal with this dish. For a lighter summer wine, look for a rosé from that region. If you prefer a red, try a Côtes de Provence.

russian-style chicken cutlets

So simple and so good—these cutlets are a case where the whole is greater than the sum of the parts. Ground chicken is often disappointingly dry, but here a bit of butter and cream keep the meat moist.

PREP TIME 5 MINUTES   **FREEZER TIME** 10 MINUTES

COOK TIME 8–10 MINUTES

SERVES 4

2	slices good-quality white bread, crusts removed
¼	cup half-and-half
1	pound ground chicken
1	egg
½	teaspoon salt
¼	teaspoon fresh-ground black pepper
½	teaspoon dried dill
5	tablespoons butter, 3 of them at room temperature
1	cup dry bread crumbs
2	tablespoons cooking oil

1. Break the bread into pieces. In a large bowl, soak the bread in the half-and-half until the liquid is absorbed, about 2 minutes. Mix in the chicken, egg, salt, pepper, dill, and the 3 tablespoons room-temperature butter. Put in the freezer for about 10 minutes to firm up.

2. Remove the chicken mixture from the freezer; it will still be very soft. Form the mixture into four oval cutlets and coat them with the bread crumbs.

3. In a large, nonstick frying pan, heat the remaining 2 tablespoons butter and the oil over moderate heat. Cook the cutlets until golden brown and just done, 4 to 5 minutes per side.

MENU SUGGESTIONS

Sautéed mushrooms are the traditional Russian accompaniment to chicken cutlets. Beets, glazed carrots, and mashed potatoes are other excellent possibilities.

VARIATION

Italian-Style Chicken Cutlets

Omit the dill. Use half bread crumbs, half grated Parmesan cheese to coat the cutlets.

wine recommendation

The butteriness of the juicy cutlets contrasts beautifully with the racy freshness of an uncomplicated red wine. A Beaujolais from France or a merlot from Trentino in Northern Italy will be perfect.

chicken livers with caramelized onions & madeira

Rich-tasting caramelized onions combined with Madeira make a spectacular sauce for chicken livers. Serve with rice or over toast so you won't miss a single drop.

PREP TIME 10 MINUTES   **COOK TIME** 20 MINUTES

SERVES 4

3	tablespoons cooking oil
3	onions, sliced thin (about 4 cups)
¾	teaspoon salt
¼	teaspoon fresh-ground black pepper
1¼	pounds chicken livers, each cut in half
½	cup Madeira
1	hard-cooked egg, chopped
2	tablespoons chopped fresh parsley

1. In a large frying pan, heat 2 tablespoons of the oil over moderate heat. Add the onions, ½ teaspoon of the salt, and ⅛ teaspoon of the pepper. Cook, stirring frequently, until the onions are well browned, about 15 minutes. Remove the onions from the pan and put on a serving platter or individual plates.

2. In the same frying pan, heat the remaining 1 tablespoon oil over moderately high heat. Season the chicken livers with the remaining ¼ teaspoon salt and ⅛ teaspoon pepper. Put the livers in the pan, in two batches if necessary, and cook for 2 minutes. Turn and cook until browned, about 2 minutes longer. The livers should still be pink inside. Remove the livers from the pan and put them on top of the onions.

3. Return the pan to the heat and add the Madeira. Boil rapidly, scraping the bottom of the pan to dislodge any brown bits, for 1 minute. Pour the sauce over the livers and the onions. Top with the egg and parsley.

VARIATIONS

Chicken Livers with Caramelized Onions & Sherry
Use ½ cup of dry sherry instead of the Madeira.

Chicken Livers with Caramelized Onions & Port
Use ½ cup of port instead of the Madeira.

wine recommendation

The rich and luscious Madeira sauce is ideal with fruity, spicy grenache-based wines. A Gigondas or a Côtes-du-Rhône from the Rhône Valley in France or a bottle of grenache from California would be appropriate.

sautéed chicken livers with raisins & pine nuts

Sicily is the inspiration for chicken livers in a wine sauce fragrant with garlic and studded with raisins and pine nuts. The livers are delicious over polenta—better yet, crisp fried polenta. Or serve them on a bed of buttered noodles or on toast.

PREP TIME 5 MINUTES   **COOK TIME** 16 MINUTES

SERVES 4

⅓   cup pine nuts

⅓   cup raisins

¾   cup canned low-sodium chicken broth or homemade stock

¾   cup dry vermouth or dry white wine

2   tablespoons butter

2   tablespoons olive oil

1¼ pounds chicken livers, each cut in half

½   teaspoon salt

¼   teaspoon fresh-ground black pepper

4   cloves garlic, minced

1½ teaspoons flour

3   tablespoons chopped flat-leaf parsley

1. Heat the oven to 350°. Toast the pine nuts in the oven until they are golden brown, about 8 minutes.

2. In a small stainless-steel saucepan, combine the raisins, broth, and vermouth. Bring to a boil and simmer until reduced to about ¾ cup, about 8 minutes. Set aside.

3. In a large frying pan, melt 1 tablespoon of the butter with 1 tablespoon of the oil over moderately high heat. Season the chicken livers with ¼ teaspoon of the salt and ⅛ teaspoon of the pepper and cook, in two batches if necessary, until almost done, about 3 minutes. The livers should still be quite pink inside. Remove them from the pan.

4. Add the remaining 1 tablespoon oil and 1 tablespoon butter to the pan and reduce the heat to moderately low. Add the garlic and cook, stirring, for 30 seconds. Add the flour and cook, stirring, for 15 seconds longer. Stir in the raisin-and-vermouth mixture and the remaining ¼ teaspoon salt and ⅛ teaspoon pepper. Bring to a simmer, scraping the bottom of the pan to dislodge any brown bits. Add the chicken livers and any accumulated juices, the pine nuts, and the parsley and simmer until the livers are just done, about 1 minute longer.

wine recommendation

Try matching the savory tastes of this Sicilian-flavored dish with a rustic red wine that hails from the same region. Or serve the easy-to-find Salice Salentino from Apulia, also in southern Italy.

turkey with bacon & greens

Thin turkey cutlets are sautéed quickly and served with tender Swiss chard and a sour-cream-based sauce. Feel free to use chicken breasts instead of turkey, or spinach in place of the Swiss chard.

PREP TIME 8 MINUTES   **COOK TIME** 20 MINUTES

SERVES 4

1½ pounds Swiss chard, long stems removed, leaves chopped and washed well
1   tablespoon water
¼   pound sliced bacon, cut into ¼-inch strips
1   onion, chopped
2   cloves garlic; chopped
4   turkey cutlets (about 1 ¼ pounds in all)
¾   teaspoon salt
¼   teaspoon fresh-ground black pepper
½   cup sour cream

1. Put the Swiss chard and the water in a medium pot. In a large nonstick frying pan, cook the bacon until crisp. Drain on paper towels. Pour off and reserve all but 1 tablespoon of the bacon fat, which you should leave in the pan.

2. Put the pan with the 1 tablespoon of fat over moderately low heat. Add the onion and cook, stirring occasionally, until translucent, about 5 minutes. Add the garlic and cook, stirring, 30 seconds longer. Add the mixture to the chard. Bring the water to a simmer, cover, and cook over low heat until the chard is wilted and tender, about 5 minutes.

3. Meanwhile, heat 2 tablespoons of the reserved bacon fat in the frying pan over moderately high heat. Season the turkey cutlets with ¼ teaspoon of the salt and the pepper. Cook until just done, 1 to 2 minutes per side. Remove the cutlets from the pan so that they don't overcook.

4. Remove the chard from the heat. Stir in the sour cream and the remaining ½ teaspoon salt. Remove the chard from the pot with a slotted spoon, leaving the sauce. Divide the chard among four plates. Top each pile of chard with a turkey cutlet. Spoon some of the sauce over the top and sprinkle with the bacon.

MENU SUGGESTIONS

Since the recipe includes a vegetable, you can finish off the meal simply with steak fries or buttered orzo.

wine recommendation

This quick sauté would be great with a fairly acidic red wine, which will cut through the richness of the bacon and match the acidity of the sour cream. Look for a Beaujolais or try a grenache-based wine from California. Serve it slightly chilled.

turkey with walnut-parmesan sauce

Ground walnuts thicken this unique sauce and give it both a subtle nuttiness and an appealing creamy texture, both of which are perfect with turkey.

PREP TIME 6 MINUTES   **COOK TIME** 12 MINUTES

SERVES 4

⅓   cup walnuts

2   tablespoons butter

½   cup chopped onion

2   cloves garlic, chopped

    Pinch ground cloves

    Pinch ground cinnamon

    Pinch cayenne

½   teaspoon salt

1½ teaspoons flour

¾   cup canned low-sodium chicken broth
    or homemade stock

½   teaspoon lemon juice

1½ tablespoons grated Parmesan cheese

2   tablespoons chopped fresh parsley

1   tablespoon cooking oil

4   turkey cutlets (about 1¼ pounds in all)

¼   teaspoon fresh-ground black pepper

1. Grind ¼ cup of the walnuts to a powder in a food processor. In a small saucepan, melt the butter over moderately low heat. Add the onion; cook until translucent, about 5 minutes. Add the garlic and cook, stirring, 30 seconds longer. Stir in the cloves, cinnamon, cayenne, and ¼ teaspoon of the salt. Add the flour and stir to combine. Whisk in the broth and simmer until starting to thicken, about 3 minutes. Add the ground walnuts and simmer 1 minute longer. Remove from the heat and stir in the lemon juice, Parmesan, and parsley.

2. In a large nonstick frying pan, heat the oil over moderately high heat. Season the turkey with the remaining ¼ teaspoon salt and the pepper. Cook the turkey cutlets until just done, 1 to 2 minutes per side. Serve with the walnut sauce, sprinkling the remaining nuts over the top.

MENU SUGGESTIONS

Roasted asparagus and sautéed peppers are two possible side dishes that would taste particularly good with both walnuts and Parmesan cheese.

wine recommendation

The walnuts will stand up to a bold red wine. Try one from the Northern Rhône in France or a California cabernet sauvignon.

Couscous Salad with
Turkey & Arugula on page 174.

6

salads & sandwiches

grilled chicken & vegetable salad with lemon & pepper vinaigrette

Cool mixed greens topped with hot grilled chicken, carrots, and shiitake mushrooms make a great light meal. You can also let the grilled vegetables and chicken cool and serve them at room temperature.

PREP TIME 10 MINUTES   **COOK TIME** 10–12 MINUTES
SERVES 4

⅓ cup plus 3 tablespoons olive oil
1 teaspoon dried thyme
1 pound boneless, skinless chicken breasts (about 3)
1 teaspoon salt
¾ teaspoon fresh-ground black pepper
¼ pound shiitake mushrooms, stems removed
4 carrots, cut diagonally into ¼-inch slices
½ teaspoon Dijon mustard
4 teaspoons lemon juice
2 heads leaf lettuce, torn into bite-size pieces (about 3 quarts)
2 scallions including green tops, chopped

1. Light the grill. In a small bowl, combine the 3 tablespoons oil and the thyme. Coat the chicken with about 1 tablespoon of the thyme oil and sprinkle with ¼ teaspoon of the salt and ⅛ teaspoon of the pepper. Grill the chicken over moderately high heat until just done, about 4 minutes per side. Remove and let rest for 5 minutes, and then cut diagonally into ¼-inch pieces.

2. In a medium bowl, toss the mushrooms and carrots with the remaining thyme oil, ¼ teaspoon of the salt, and ⅛ teaspoon of the pepper. Grill the vegetables over moderately high heat, turning, until just done, about 4 minutes per side for the carrots and 6 minutes per side for the mushrooms.

3. In a small glass or stainless-steel bowl, whisk together the mustard, lemon juice, and the remaining ½ teaspoon salt and ½ teaspoon pepper. Whisk in the remaining ⅓ cup oil.

4. In a large bowl, combine the lettuce, half of the scallions, and all but 2 tablespoons of the vinaigrette. Mound onto plates. Top with the vegetables and chicken. Drizzle the remaining vinaigrette over the chicken and top with the remaining scallions.

wine recommendation

Look for a wine that has plenty of acidity to stand up to the vinaigrette. In the warmer months, a white such as a California sauvignon blanc or an Italian pinot grigio will taste best. If you prefer a red wine, try a gamay or pinot noir from California.

vietnamese chicken salad

Bold flavors star in this Vietnamese salad—acidic lime juice, hot pepper, salty soy sauce, and cooling herbs. The combination of mint and cilantro is typical and refreshing, but you can use only one herb, or leave them both out completely if you prefer.

PREP TIME 12 MINUTES   **COOK TIME** 10 MINUTES
SERVES 4

1⅓	pounds boneless, skinless chicken breasts (about 4)
1	cup canned low-sodium chicken broth or homemade stock
4	scallions including green tops, chopped
½	teaspoon salt
1¼	pounds green cabbage (about ½ head), shredded (about 4 cups)
3	carrots, grated
6	tablespoons chopped fresh mint and/or cilantro (optional)
¼	cup lime juice (from about 2 limes)
¼	cup soy sauce or Asian fish sauce (nam pla or nuoc mam)*
4	teaspoons sugar
¼	teaspoon dried red-pepper flakes
¼	cup chopped peanuts

*Available at Asian markets and some supermarkets

1. Cut each chicken breast into five diagonal strips. In a medium saucepan, combine the broth, ¼ of the scallions, and ¼ teaspoon of the salt. Bring to a simmer, add the chicken, stir, and cover the pan. Cook over low heat for 5 minutes. Turn the heat off and let the chicken steam for 5 minutes. Remove the chicken from the pan and shred it.

2. In a large bowl, combine the shredded chicken, the remaining scallions, the cabbage, carrots, and 4 tablespoons of the herbs, if using. In a small glass or stainless-steel bowl, whisk together the lime juice, soy sauce, sugar, red-pepper flakes, and the remaining ¼ teaspoon salt. Toss the salad with the dressing. Sprinkle with the remaining 2 tablespoons chopped herbs and the peanuts.

MENU SUGGESTIONS

This crunchy, Asian-flavored salad will taste even more refreshing served with tropical fruit, such as pineapple, mango, papaya, or star fruit.

wine recommendation

A lively, acidic white wine that has no oak flavor will be best with the spices and greens in this dish. Try a sauvignon blanc from South Africa or Australia or a pinot grigio from Italy.

spinach salad with smoked chicken, apple, walnuts, & bacon

Celebrate autumn's apple season with this delicious and satisfying salad. We call for the thick-sliced smoked chicken now available in the meat department of supermarkets. Of course, you can always use smoked turkey from the deli counter instead. If you like a more pronounced sweet-and-sour flavor, use another teaspoon of vinegar.

PREP TIME 15 MINUTES **COOK TIME** 8–10 MINUTES
SERVES 4

¾	cup walnuts, chopped
¼	pound sliced bacon
2	tablespoons red-wine vinegar
1	teaspoon Dijon mustard
¾	teaspoon salt
¼	teaspoon fresh-ground black pepper
⅓	cup cooking oil
⅔	pound smoked and sliced boneless chicken breast
1	pound spinach, stems removed, leaves washed (about 9 cups)
1	small red onion, chopped fine
1	tart apple, such as Granny Smith, peeled, cored, and cut into ½-inch pieces

1. Heat the oven to 350°. Toast the walnuts until golden brown, about 8 minutes. Let cool.

2. In a large frying pan, cook the bacon until it is crisp. Drain the bacon on paper towels and then crumble it.

3. In a small glass or stainless-steel bowl, whisk the vinegar with the mustard, salt, and pepper. Whisk in the oil.

4. In a large bowl, combine 2 tablespoons of the dressing with the chicken. Let sit for about 5 minutes so that the chicken absorbs the dressing. Add the walnuts, bacon, spinach, onion, apple, and the remaining dressing and toss.

MENU SUGGESTIONS
Warm garlic bread, served either plain or with a little Parmesan cheese, goes well with all the flavors here.

wine recommendation

This substantial fall salad, with its hearty flavors, will taste great with a Beaujolais or, for something off the beaten path, a fruity pinotage from South Africa. In either case, chill the bottle for fifteen minutes or so before serving.

sesame chicken salad

Sesame sauce bathes layers of chicken, cucumber, and noodles in this satisfying main-course salad. Assemble the salad just before serving, or the cucumbers will release liquid, turn limp, and make the sauce watery.

PREP TIME 12 MINUTES   **STEAM TIME** 5 MINUTES
COOK TIME 10 MINUTES
SERVES 4

¼	pound vermicelli
1	cup plus 3 tablespoons canned low-sodium chicken broth or homemade stock
3	scallions including green tops, cut into ¼-inch slices
¼	teaspoon salt
1⅓	pounds boneless, skinless chicken breasts (about 4)
1	tablespoon chopped fresh ginger
4	cloves garlic, chopped
2	tablespoons tahini (sesame-seed paste)
1	tablespoon Asian sesame oil
2	teaspoons sugar
2½	tablespoons cooking oil
⅛	teaspoon dried red-pepper flakes
3	tablespoons soy sauce
½	teaspoon fresh-ground black pepper
2	cucumbers, halved lengthwise, peeled, and seeded

1. In a pot of boiling, salted water, cook the vermicelli until just done, about 9 minutes. Drain. Rinse with cold water; drain thoroughly.

2. In a medium saucepan, combine the 1 cup broth, one third of the scallions, and the salt. Bring to a simmer, add the chicken, stir, and cover the pan. Simmer for 5 minutes. Turn the heat off and let the chicken steam for 5 minutes. Remove the chicken from the saucepan and shred it.

3. In a blender, puree the remaining 3 tablespoons broth, the ginger, garlic, tahini, sesame oil, sugar, cooking oil, red-pepper flakes, soy sauce, and pepper. Put the cucumber halves cut-side down and slice them lengthwise into thin strips.

4. To serve, put the vermicelli on plates or in bowls. Scatter each serving with a layer of cucumber strips and then top with the shredded chicken. Pour the sesame sauce over the chicken and sprinkle with the remaining scallions.

wine recommendation

The bold flavors of the salad will be complemented by the acidity and slight sweetness of a German kabinett riesling from the Mosel-Saar-Ruwer.

moroccan chicken & potato salad with olives

A savory lemon dressing with cumin, paprika, ginger, and oregano gives this salad an exotic flavor. Serve the salad warm or at room temperature.

PREP TIME 10 MINUTES   **COOK TIME** 25 MINUTES
SERVES 4

1½	pounds boiling potatoes (about 5)
1½	tablespoons lemon juice
1	teaspoon ground cumin
1	teaspoon paprika
1	teaspoon salt
	Fresh-ground black pepper
¼	teaspoon ground ginger
¼	teaspoon dried oregano
7	tablespoons olive oil
1	pound boneless, skinless chicken breasts (about 3)
½	red onion, chopped fine
⅓	cup black olives, such as Kalamata, halved and pitted
½	cup chopped flat-leaf parsley

1. Put the potatoes in a medium saucepan with salted water to cover and bring to a boil. Reduce the heat and cook at a gentle boil until tender, about 25 minutes. Drain the potatoes. When they are cool enough to handle, peel the potatoes and cut into ¼-inch slices.

2. Meanwhile, in a small glass or stainless-steel bowl, whisk together the lemon juice, cumin, paprika, ¾ teaspoon of the salt, ¼ teaspoon pepper, the ginger, and the oregano. Whisk in 6 tablespoons of the oil.

3. Heat a grill pan or a heavy frying pan over moderate heat. For the grill pan, coat the chicken with the remaining 1 tablespoon oil; sprinkle with the remaining ¼ teaspoon salt and ⅛ teaspoon pepper. Cook the chicken for 5 minutes. Turn and cook until browned and just done, about 4 minutes longer. Remove, and when cool enough to handle, cut the chicken into ¼-inch slices. For the frying pan, heat the oil in the pan and then season, cook, and slice the chicken in the same way.

4. In a large bowl, combine the warm potatoes with half of the dressing. Add the chicken, onion, olives, parsley, and the remaining dressing and toss.

wine recommendation

This dish would be wonderful with a well-chilled bottle of rosé, which will refresh the palate without interfering with the salad's flavors. Look for a bottle from Bandol, Cassis, or elsewhere in the South of France.

southwestern tortilla salad

This Tex-Mex favorite comes together in minutes. You'll be surprised by how quick and easy it is to make your own refried beans—and how much better they taste than the ready-made variety.

PREP TIME 10 MINUTES   **COOK TIME** 8–10 MINUTES
SERVES 4

8	taco shells
5½	tablespoons cooking oil
2	cups drained and rinsed kidney beans (from one 19-ounce can)
⅓	cup tomato salsa
¾	teaspoon salt
1½	tablespoons wine vinegar
¼	teaspoon Dijon mustard
¼	teaspoon fresh-ground black pepper
¼	teaspoon chili powder
¼	cup chopped cilantro (optional)
1	head romaine lettuce, shredded
2	large tomatoes, chopped
1	avocado, cut into thin slices
¼	pound cheddar cheese, grated (about 1 cup)
1	roasted chicken, bones and skin removed, meat shredded (about 1 pound meat)
⅓	cup black olives, such as Kalamata, halved and pitted

1. Heat the oven to 350°. Put the taco shells on a baking sheet and bake them until crisp, about 8 minutes. Break each one in half.

2. In a medium saucepan, heat 1 tablespoon of the oil over moderate heat. Add the beans, salsa, and ¼ teaspoon of the salt. Cook, mashing with a potato masher, for about 5 minutes.

3. In a small glass or stainless-steel bowl, whisk together the vinegar, mustard, pepper, chili powder, and the remaining ½ teaspoon salt. Add the remaining 4½ tablespoons oil, whisking. Add the cilantro.

4. To serve, spread one side of the taco-shell halves with the refried beans and put four on each plate. Top with layers of the lettuce, tomatoes, avocado, cheese, chicken, and olives. Pour the dressing over the salads.

wine recommendation

The forceful flavor of cheddar cheese and the saltiness of the olives will go very nicely with a crisp and lively sauvignon blanc from California.

chicken burritos with black-bean salsa & pepper jack

Pepper Jack cheese looks innocent enough but adds a nice kick to these burritos. If you prefer a milder taste, use regular Jack instead.

PREP TIME 6 MINUTES   **COOK TIME** 20-25 MINUTES
SERVES 4

1⅔ cups drained and rinsed black beans
     (from one 15-ounce can)
2   scallions including green tops, chopped
1   tablespoon lemon or lime juice
¼   teaspoon ground cumin
½   teaspoon salt
1⅓ pounds boneless, skinless chicken breasts
     (about 4)
¼   teaspoon chili powder
¼   teaspoon fresh-ground black pepper
½   pound pepper Jack cheese, grated
4   large (9-inch) flour tortillas

1. Light the grill or heat the broiler. In a small glass or stainless-steel bowl, combine the beans, scallions, lemon juice, cumin, and ¼ teaspoon of the salt.

2. Rub the chicken breasts with the chili powder, pepper, and the remaining ¼ teaspoon salt. Cook the chicken over moderate heat for 5 minutes. Turn and cook until brown and just done, 4 to 5 minutes longer. Remove, let the chicken rest for a few minutes, and then slice.

3. Heat the oven to 350°. Put one quarter of the cheese in a line near one edge of each tortilla. Top the cheese with one quarter of the black-bean salsa and then with one quarter of the chicken slices. Roll up the burritos and wrap each one in foil. Bake them until the cheese melts, about 15 minutes.

DO-AHEAD TIP
You can assemble the burritos ahead of time and bake them just before serving. If they've been in the refrigerator, add about 5 minutes to the baking time.

MENU SUGGESTIONS
Embellish your burritos with sour cream or salsa, if you like. Sliced tomatoes or rice would make good side dishes.

wine recommendation

With the heat from the cheese, stay away from any serious, high-alcohol, low-acid wines. Try a white from a cooler growing area such as a riesling from the Finger Lakes region of New York or any white from the Alto Adige region of Italy. A cold beer is a great alternative.

chicken & feta tostadas

A Mexican classic with a Greek twist, these tostadas appeal to children of all ages. If you can't buy roasted chicken ready-made, use leftover chicken or cook some according to whichever of the methods on pages 180 to 181 seems easiest to you. Serve one burrito-size tortilla or two of the smaller ones per person.

PREP TIME 10 MINUTES   **COOK TIME** 5–7 MINUTES
SERVES 4

- ¾ pound plum tomatoes, chopped
- ½ cup black olives, such as Kalamata, pitted and chopped
- ¼ cup chopped fresh parsley
- 1 roasted chicken, bones and skin removed, meat shredded (about 1 pound boneless meat)
- ½ teaspoon salt
- ½ teaspoon fresh-ground black pepper
- 2 tablespoons red-wine vinegar
- 3 tablespoons cooking oil, plus more for brushing tortillas
- 8 small or 4 large flour tortillas
- ½ pound feta cheese, crumbled (about 2 cups)

1. Heat the oven to 450°. In a large glass or stainless-steel bowl, combine the tomatoes, olives, parsley, chicken, salt, pepper, vinegar, and the 3 tablespoons oil.

2. Brush the tortillas on both sides with oil and then put on baking sheets, overlapping if necessary. Bake the tortillas until starting to brown, 2 to 3 minutes. Turn the tortillas and brown the other side, 2 to 3 minutes longer.

3. Remove the baking sheets from the oven and top each tortilla with an equal amount of the feta cheese. Return the baking sheets to the oven; cook until the cheese is just melting, 1 to 2 minutes longer. Top the tortillas with the chicken mixture.

MENU SUGGESTIONS
A fruit salad would be an easy and complementary accompaniment.

wine recommendation

The saltiness of the feta cheese and olives and the tartness of the tomatoes will pair well with the crisp acidity in a sauvignon blanc from either the Loire Valley or a northern region of Italy such as Collio or Veneto.

chicken souvlaki

Grilled chicken on pita with tomatoes, onions, and tzatziki, a yogurt and cucumber sauce, makes a cool yet satisfying warm-weather supper. Souvlaki is often rolled to eat in your hand as a snack, but this more substantial version is served on a plate with a knife and fork. If you like, accompany the souvlaki with lemon wedges. When using wooden skewers, soak them first in water for at least ten minutes, or they'll smoke during cooking.

PREP TIME 10 MINUTES   **COOK TIME** 5 MINUTES

REST TIME 15 MINUTES

SERVES 4

2   cups plain yogurt

1   cucumber, halved lengthwise, peeled, seeded, and grated

1¼ teaspoons salt

1   clove garlic, minced
    Fresh-ground black pepper

¼   teaspoon dried dill

2   tablespoons olive oil

1½ teaspoons lemon juice

1   tablespoon dried oregano

1⅓ pounds boneless, skinless chicken breasts (about 4), cut into 1-inch cubes

4   pocketless pitas

6   tablespoons butter, at room temperature

1   small onion, cut into thin wedges

2   tomatoes, cut into thin wedges

⅓   cup black olives, such as Kalamata, halved and pitted

1. Put the yogurt in a strainer lined with cheesecloth, a coffee filter, or a paper towel and set it over a bowl. Let drain in the refrigerator for 15 minutes. In a medium glass or stainless-steel bowl, combine the cucumber with 1 teaspoon of the salt; let sit for about 15 minutes. Squeeze the cucumber to remove the liquid. Put the cucumber back in the bowl and stir in the drained yogurt, the garlic, ⅛ teaspoon of pepper, and the dill.

2. Light the grill or heat the broiler. In a small glass or stainless-steel bowl, combine the oil, lemon juice, oregano, the remaining ¼ teaspoon of salt, and ¼ teaspoon of pepper. Toss the chicken cubes in the oil mixture and thread them onto skewers. Grill the chicken over high heat or broil, turning once, until done, about 5 minutes in all. Transfer the chicken to a plate.

3. Spread both sides of the pitas with the butter and grill or broil, turning once, until golden, about 4 minutes in all. Cut into quarters.

4. To serve, put the pitas on plates and top with the onion, tomatoes, and chicken skewers with any accumulated juices. Serve with the tzatziki and olives.

wine recommendation

This traditional Greek preparation goes with a number of choices to suit the occasion and your taste. Look for a very fruity red such as a Beaujolais, a sparkling wine from California, or a sauvignon blanc from northern Italy.

spicy pita pockets with chicken, lentils, & tahini sauce

Here's something great to do with roasted chicken from the deli—a Middle Eastern sandwich chock-full of spicy lentils, bulgur, lettuce, tomato, and tahini sauce. Two pockets per person is enough to make a meal. If you like, serve extra Tabasco sauce at the table. You can find tahini (sesame-seed paste) in most supermarkets.

PREP TIME 10 MINUTES   **COOK TIME** 25-30 MINUTES

REST TIME 5 MINUTES

SERVES 4

1	cup dried lentils
½	onion, cut in half
2¾	cups plus 6 tablespoons water
1	tablespoon olive oil
2½	teaspoons salt
1	bay leaf
½	cup coarse bulgur
1½	teaspoons Tabasco sauce
½	cup tahini
2	cloves garlic, minced
5	teaspoons lemon juice
1	cup plain yogurt
8	pitas
1	roasted chicken, bones and skin removed, meat shredded (about 1 pound meat)
2	large tomatoes, chopped
1	head romaine lettuce, shredded

1. Heat the oven to 350°. In a medium saucepan, combine the lentils, onion, the 2¾ cups water, the oil, 1 teaspoon of the salt, and the bay leaf. Bring to a boil; simmer, partially covered, for 15 minutes. Stir in the bulgur and continue cooking, partially covered, stirring occasionally, until the lentils and bulgur are just done, about 12 more minutes. Remove from the heat, stir in the Tabasco sauce, and let sit, partially covered, for 5 minutes. Remove the onion and the bay leaf.

2. Meanwhile, in a medium glass or stainless-steel bowl, whisk together the tahini, the remaining 6 tablespoons water, the garlic, the lemon juice, the remaining 1½ teaspoons salt, and the yogurt.

3. Wrap the pitas in aluminum foil and warm them in the oven, about 10 minutes.

4. Cut the top third off of each pita. Spoon ¼ cup of the lentil mixture into each pita. Divide half the chicken and tomatoes among the pitas and drizzle each with 1 tablespoon of the sauce. Top with half the lettuce. Repeat. Serve with the remaining sauce.

wine recommendation

You need a straightforward wine that won't compete but will be gulpable enough to prepare the palate for the next hot bite. Try a chenin blanc or a white zinfandel from California.

chicken pan bagnat

Literally "bathed bread" in the ancient dialect of Provence, pan bagnat delivers meat, bread, and salad all in one handful. You both brush the bread with oil and let the finished rolls sit for a few minutes to allow the dressing to permeate the bread and "bathe" it with flavor.

PREP TIME 12–15 MINUTES   **NO COOKING**

REST TIME, OPTIONAL 10 MINUTES

SERVES 4

1	tablespoon lemon juice
2	teaspoons chopped fresh thyme, or ¾ teaspoon dried thyme
¾	teaspoon salt
¾	teaspoon fresh-ground black pepper
⅓	cup plus 2 tablespoons olive oil
4	large, crusty rolls, cut in half
1	large clove garlic, cut in half
8	large, crisp lettuce leaves, such as Boston
2	large tomatoes, sliced thin
1	roasted chicken, bones and skin removed, meat shredded (about 1 pound meat)
2	hard-cooked eggs, sliced
1	red onion, sliced thin
1	green bell pepper, sliced thin
⅓	cup black olives, such as Kalamata, halved and pitted
8	anchovy fillets (optional)

1. In a small glass or stainless-steel bowl, whisk together the lemon juice, thyme, ½ teaspoon each of the salt and pepper. Whisk in the ⅓ cup of oil.

2. Remove the soft centers of the rolls, leaving a ½-inch shell. Rub the garlic on the inside of each and brush with the 2 tablespoons oil.

3. Top the bottoms of the rolls with the lettuce. Layer with half the tomato slices and the chicken; sprinkle with ⅛ teaspoon each of salt and pepper. Top with half the slices of egg, onion, and bell pepper, and half the olives, and then drizzle with half the dressing. Repeat with the remaining tomato, chicken, ⅛ teaspoon each salt and pepper, egg, onion, bell pepper, olives, and dressing. Top with the anchovies, if using. Cover with the tops of the rolls. If you have time, wrap each roll tightly in aluminum foil; let sit for 10 minutes. Otherwise, press down on the rolls firmly so that the dressing moistens the bread.

MENU SUGGESTIONS

You really don't need anything with this, but roasted potato wedges or fancy potato chips would be nice.

wine recommendation

The south-of-France flavor of this sandwich is perfect with the delicate, herbal notes found in many rosés from Provence. Bottles from the Coteaux du Varois, Cassis, or Bandol would all be good possibilities.

turkey burgers

The focaccia adds to the Italian flavor of these juicy burgers. However, bread selections are endless—toasted country bread, onion rolls, or whatever you like.

PREP TIME 8 MINUTES   **COOK TIME** 10–12 MINUTES
SERVES 4

1½ pounds ground turkey
¼ cup dry bread crumbs
¼ cup grated Parmesan cheese
¼ cup chopped fresh parsley
2 scallions including green tops, chopped
   Salt
¼ teaspoon fresh-ground black pepper
2 tablespoons milk
1 egg, beaten to mix
2 tablespoons cooking oil
¼ pound provolone cheese, sliced
½ cup mayonnaise
3 tablespoons pesto, store-bought or homemade
1 10-inch round or 8-by-10-inch rectangle of focaccia
½ pound tomatoes, sliced

1. In a medium bowl, combine the ground turkey, bread crumbs, Parmesan cheese, parsley, scallions, ¾ teaspoon salt, the pepper, milk, and egg. Form the mixture into four patties, each about 1 inch thick.

2. In a large nonstick frying pan, heat the oil over moderate heat. Add the turkey burgers and cook for 5 minutes. Turn and then top each burger with the provolone cheese. Cook until just done, about 6 minutes longer.

3. Meanwhile, in a small bowl, combine the mayonnaise and the pesto. Cut the focaccia into quarters. Cut each piece in half horizontally. Spread the cut surfaces of each piece with the pesto mayonnaise.

4. Top the bottoms of the focaccia with the turkey burgers and then the tomato slices. Sprinkle the tomato with a pinch of salt. Cover with the top piece of focaccia.

MENU SUGGESTIONS

Burgers go best with other finger food—oven-roasted potato wedges and raw carrot or fennel sticks, for example.

wine recommendation

This meaty sandwich should be paired with a fresh, full-flavored red, perhaps one made from the versatile, food-friendly barbera grape. Several are imported from Italy's Piedmont region.

smoked turkey & slaw on country toast

A simple slaw complements deli turkey in this tempting sandwich. Experiment with different breads, such as toasted sourdough, rye, or pita.

PREP TIME 8 MINUTES   **COOK TIME** 4–5 MINUTES
SERVES 4

12	tablespoons wine vinegar
1	pound red cabbage (about ⅓ head), shredded (about 1 quart)
2	carrots, grated
½	cup mayonnaise
¼	teaspoon ground cumin
¼	teaspoon paprika
¼	teaspoon salt
¼	teaspoon fresh-ground black pepper
8	thick slices from 1 large round loaf of country bread
1	pound smoked turkey, sliced thin
1	pound tomatoes, sliced

1. In a medium stainless-steel saucepan, heat the vinegar over moderate heat. Add the red cabbage and toss until it is starting to wilt, 1 to 2 minutes. Transfer the cabbage to a medium glass or stainless-steel bowl and toss with the carrots, mayonnaise, cumin, paprika, salt, and pepper.

2. Heat the broiler. Put the bread on a baking sheet and broil, turning once, until crisp on the outside but still slightly soft in the center, about 3 minutes in all. Sandwich the turkey, sliced tomato, and slaw between pieces of toast.

MENU SUGGESTIONS

Sandwiches need simple, no-fuss companions, such as oven fries, chips, or fruit salad.

VARIATIONS

Embellish the slaw as you like. Chopped scallions, grated jicama, or thin slices of green pepper all make good additions.

wine recommendation

Serve a simple, flavorful wine, such as a barrel-fermented sauvignon blanc from California or a pinot blanc from Alsace in France.

couscous salad with turkey & arugula

Sweet raisins, crunchy nuts, spicy arugula—this couscous salad boasts an interesting array of flavors and textures. We include strips of roasted or smoked turkey to make it a meal, but you can leave them out for a meatless salad.

PREP TIME 8 MINUTES   **COOK TIME** 5 MINUTES
REST TIME 5 MINUTES
SERVES 4

2	cups water
1	teaspoon salt
1⅓	cups couscous
⅓	cup raisins
⅓	cup walnuts
¼	cup lemon juice (from about 1 lemon)
½	teaspoon fresh-ground black pepper
6	tablespoons olive oil
2	carrots, grated
1	½-pound piece cooked turkey, cut crosswise into thin strips
5	ounces arugula, tough stems removed, leaves washed and chopped (about 3 cups)

1. In a medium saucepan, bring the water and ½ teaspoon of the salt to a boil. Stir in the couscous and raisins. Cover, remove from the heat, and let stand for 5 minutes. Transfer the couscous and raisins to a large bowl to cool.

2. Meanwhile, in a small frying pan, toast the walnuts over moderately low heat, stirring frequently, until golden brown, about 5 minutes. Or toast the nuts in a 350° oven for 10 minutes. Remove the nuts from the pan and chop them.

3. In a large glass or stainless-steel bowl, whisk together the lemon juice, ¼ teaspoon of the salt, and the pepper. Add the oil slowly, whisking constantly.

4. Toss the carrots, the toasted nuts, the turkey, the arugula, and the remaining ¼ teaspoon salt with the cooled couscous. Toss the salad with the dressing.

VARIATION

Couscous Salad with Turkey & Watercress or Spinach Leaves
Substitute 3 cups of shredded watercress or spinach leaves for the arugula.

wine recommendation

It may surprise you to learn that Germany and Austria make good red wines, racy with brilliantly pure berry flavors. Look for Germany's dornfelder or Austria's Zweigelt for a brisk change of pace.

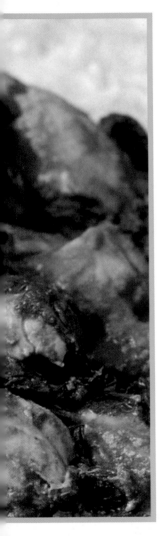

7

multiply your options

Look to this section for practical help in deciding what ingredients to keep on hand, choosing the easiest way to cook your chicken, and planning how to serve it. Among the useful guides, you'll find ideas for making salads and simply sauced dishes and, for those times when you can't think what to do with the remainders of a roast chicken or turkey, a list of recipes in which you can include leftovers.

the quick pantry

If you keep basic staples on hand, you can cut shopping to a minimum.
Then you'll only have to make one short stop to pick up the fresh vegetables
and poultry you need to complete the recipe.

CUPBOARD

- apple cider or
  juice
- apricots, dried
- beans, canned:
  black, chickpeas,
  kidney, white
- bread crumbs
- bulgur
- chicken broth,
  low-sodium
- coconut milk,
  unsweetened
- couscous
- figs, dried
- garlic
- grits,
  old-fashioned
- honey
- lentils
- maple syrup
- oil: cooking, olive
- onions
- pasta, dried:
  various shapes
- peanut butter
- pimientos
- potatoes
- raisins
- rice: arborio,
  long- or
  medium-grain
- soy sauce
- Tabasco sauce
- taco shells
- tomatoes: canned,
  paste, sun-dried
- vinegar: balsamic,
  red- or white-wine,
  rice-wine

SPICE SHELF

- allspice
- bay leaves
- cayenne
- chili powder
- cinnamon
- cloves
- coriander, ground
  and seeds
- cumin
- curry powder
- dill
- five-spice powder
- ginger
- marjoram
- mustard, dry
- nutmeg
- oregano
- paprika
- red-pepper flakes
- rosemary
- sage
- sesame seeds
- tarragon
- thyme
- turmeric

LIQUOR CABINET

- bourbon
- brandy
- port
- sherry
- vermouth, dry
  white

FREEZER

- bacon
- frozen vegetables:
  Brussels sprouts,
  okra, spinach
- nuts: peanuts, pine
  nuts, walnuts
- pasta

REFRIGERATOR

- anchovy paste
- apples
- butter
- capers
- cheese:
  Parmesan
- cream
- eggs
- fish sauce, Asian
- ginger, fresh
- jalapeño peppers
- ketchup
- lemon
- limes
- mayonnaise
- mustard: Dijon
  or grainy
- olives:
  black, green
- oranges
- parsley
- pesto
- salsa
- scallions
- sesame oil, Asian
- sour cream
- tahini
- yogurt, plain

leftovers

You can use leftover chicken or turkey in any of the recipes listed here. Substitute either one for the poultry called for in the ingredient list and add the meat when the dish is almost finished so that it just reheats rather than overcooks.

Soups, Stews, Curries & Other Braised Dishes
- Kale & Potato Soup with Turkey Sausage, page 18
- Spicy Chicken Chili, page 20
- Indian-Spiced Chicken & Spinach, page 26
- Massaman Curry, page 28
- Chicken Thighs with Lentils, Chorizo, & Red Pepper, page 38

Pasta & Grains:
- Chicken Breasts with Orzo, Carrots, Dill, & Avgolemono Sauce, page 46
- Orecchiette with Chicken, Caramelized Onions, & Blue Cheese, page 48
- Fusilli with Spicy Chicken Sausage, Tomato, & Ricotta Cheese, page 50
- Chicken Pad Thai, page 52
- Mushroom & Chicken Risotto, page 58
- Risotto with Smoked Turkey, Leeks, & Mascarpone, page 60
- Turkey Sausage with Cheddar-Cheese Grits & Tomato Sauce, page 66

Roasted, Baked, & Grilled:
- Chicken & Eggplant Parmesan, page 102
- Grilled Chicken with Spicy Brazilian Tomato & Coconut Sauce, page 112

Sautés & Stir-Fries:
- Sautéed Chicken Breasts with Fennel & Rosemary, page 126
- Kung Pao Chicken, page 130
- Cashew Chicken, page 130 (variation)
- Stir-Fried Chicken with Chinese Cabbage, page 132
- Turkey with Bacon & Greens, page 142
- Turkey with Walnut-Parmesan Sauce, page 144

Salads & Sandwiches:
- Grilled Chicken & Vegetable Salad with Lemon & Pepper Vinaigrette, page 148
- Vietnamese Chicken Salad, page 150
- Spinach Salad with Smoked Chicken, Apple, Walnuts, & Bacon, page 152
- Moroccan Chicken & Potato Salad with Olives, page 156
- Southwestern Tortilla Salad, page 158
- Chicken Burritos with Black-Bean Salsa & Pepper Jack, page 160
- Chicken & Feta Tostadas, page 162
- Spicy Pita Pockets with Chicken, Lentils, & Tahini Sauce, page 166
- Chicken Pan Bagnat, page 168
- Smoked Turkey & Slaw on Country Toast, page 172

basic chicken-cooking methods

Some of our recipes call for store-bought roast chicken. If you'd rather cook your own, use any of the following methods. You'll find these recipes handy not only when you need cooked meat but when you want to serve plain chicken, embellish it with a pan sauce or compound butter, or make chicken salad (see pages 182 and 183).

Roasted Whole Chicken

1 chicken (3 to 3½ pounds)
½ teaspoon salt
¼ teaspoon fresh-ground black pepper
1 tablespoon cooking oil

Heat the oven 425°. Rub the bird inside and out with the salt and pepper. Twist the wings behind the back; tie the legs together. Put the chicken, breast-side up, in a roasting pan. Coat the chicken with the oil. Roast the chicken until done, about 55 minutes. Let the bird rest at least 10 minutes before cutting.

Individual Servings

These recipes render about 1 pound of chicken meat. If you are serving individual pieces to four people, increase the number of thighs from six to eight, or replace the thighs with four whole legs. Add a few more minutes cooking time if you use legs.

Bone-In Breasts or Thighs

BAKED

4	bone-in chicken breasts or 6 thighs
1	tablespoon cooking oil
¼	teaspoon salt
⅛	teaspoon fresh-ground black pepper

Heat the oven to 400°. Coat the chicken with the oil; season with the salt and pepper. Put the chicken, skin-side up, in a roasting pan. Bake until just done, about 25 minutes for the breasts and 30 minutes for the thighs.

GRILLED

4	bone-in chicken breasts or 6 thighs
3	tablespoon cooking oil
¼	teaspoon salt
⅛	teaspoon fresh-ground black pepper

Light the grill. Coat the chicken with 1 tablespoon of the oil and season with the salt and pepper. Grill over moderately high heat, basting with the remaining 2 tablespoons oil, until just done, about 10 minutes per side for breasts and 12 per side for thighs.

POACHED

2	cups canned low-sodium chicken broth or homemade stock
½	teaspoon salt
4	bone-in chicken breasts or 6 thighs

In a large frying pan, combine the broth and salt and bring to a simmer. Add the chicken in a single layer and simmer, covered, for 10 minutes for breasts, 15 for thighs. Remove the pan from the heat. Let the chicken steam until just done, about 5 minutes, and remove from the broth. Strain the flavorful broth for later use.

Boneless, Skinless Breasts or Thighs

SAUTÉED

1	tablespoon cooking oil
4	boneless, skinless chicken breasts, or 6 boneless, skinless thighs
¼	teaspoon salt
⅛	teaspoon fresh-ground black pepper

In a large nonstick frying pan, heat the oil over moderate heat. Season the chicken with the salt and pepper, add to the pan, and cook until brown, about 5 minutes. Turn and cook until almost done, about 3 minutes longer for breasts and 5 for thighs. Cover the pan, remove from the heat, and let steam 5 minutes.

GRILLED

4	boneless, skinless chicken breasts, or 6 boneless, skinless thighs
3	tablespoons cooking oil
¼	teaspoon salt
⅛	teaspoon fresh-ground black pepper

Light the grill. Coat the chicken with 1 tablespoon of the oil and season with the salt and pepper. Grill the chicken over moderately high heat, basting with the remaining 2 tablespoons oil, until just done, about 5 minutes per side for breasts and 7 minutes per side for thighs.

POACHED

2	cups canned low-sodium chicken broth or homemade stock
½	teaspoon salt
4	boneless, skinless chicken breasts, or 6 boneless, skinless thighs

In a large frying pan, combine the broth and salt and bring to a simmer. Add the chicken in a single layer and simmer, covered, for 5 minutes for breasts, 10 for thighs. Remove the pan from the heat, let the chicken steam for 5 minutes longer, and remove from the broth. Strain the flavorful broth for later use.

infinite possibilities

pan sauces

An easy way to make a quick meal is to sauté your favorite chicken parts and finish them off with a simple pan sauce. The technique is easy; just adapt it to what you like and have on hand.

1. **SAUTÉ** chicken in a little oil or a combination of oil and butter. Remove chicken from the pan.
2. **ADD** aromatic vegetables and cook until starting to soften. For a simpler sauce, skip this step.
3. **DEGLAZE** the pan with a flavorful liquid or combination of liquids: Bring to a boil, scraping the bottom of the pan to dislodge any browned bits. Boil until reduced to half the original quantity.
4. **THICKEN** the sauce. Add a thickening ingredient and simmer for 2 minutes (optional.)
5. **SEASON** the sauce with salt, pepper, and your flavoring(s) of choice.

sample combinations

French	*Italian*	*Southwestern*
1. Sauté chicken.	1. Sauté chicken.	1. Sauté chicken.
2. Add shallot.	2. Add garlic.	2. Add red bell pepper.
3. Deglaze with vermouth and chicken stock.	3. Deglaze with red wine.	3. Deglaze with chicken stock.
4. Thicken with butter.	4. Thicken with tomato puree.	4. Thicken with half-and-half.
5. Season with chopped tarragon.	5. Season with capers and chopped basil.	5. Season with chopped cilantro and a little lime juice.

compound butters

Compound butters melt to make the simplest of sauces for grilled, baked, broiled, or sautéed chicken (see pages 180 to 181). Start with softened butter and stir in any of the following, or almost anything else you like; you can also use a food processor to combine. Season with salt and pepper. Use the butter immediately or make it ahead, roll it into a log, freeze it, and cut off slices as you need them to top hot chicken.

- Parsley and lemon juice
- Pine nuts, basil, and sun-dried tomatoes
- Lemon zest and crushed black peppercorns
- Soy sauce and chopped scallion
- Capers and anchovy paste
- Pecans and maple syrup
- Orange zest and cayenne pepper

- Tarragon
- Chipotle chiles, lime juice, and cilantro
- Calvados and walnuts
- Olives and crushed fennel seed
- Garlic and sage
- Red wine and roasted red pepper
- Basil and mint

chicken salads

Don't ignore chicken salad as a basic of the quick-dinner repertoire. Serve warm or at room temperature with raw vegetables or on bread. Use leftover chicken, store-bought roasted chicken, or chicken just cooked by one of our easy Basic Cooking Methods (see pages 180 to 181) and add one of the possibilities below—or ingredients of your choice.

For creamy chicken salad, mix cooked, cut-up chicken with mayonnaise, sour cream, yogurt, or a combination of these. Season with salt and pepper to taste. If you like, add:

- Parmesan cheese and lemon juice
- Dijon mustard and dill
- Pesto and cherry tomatoes
- Watercress and cucumber
- Fennel and walnuts
- Avocado, cayenne, and lime juice
- Red onion and tarragon

For a lighter chicken salad, toss the meat with a vinaigrette made from three or four parts oil to one part vinegar and seasoned with salt and pepper. If you like, add:

- Green beans and scallions
- Bean sprouts, carrots, and sesame oil
- Bell pepper and oregano
- Artichoke hearts and lemon juice
- Radicchio and sun-dried tomatoes
- Smoked mozzarella and asparagus
- Pear and a touch of curry powder

index

a

ALTO ADIGE, WHITE, *recommended with*
    chicken burritos with black-bean salsa
      and pepper Jack, 160
ANCHOVY PASTE, in grilled Cornish hens with
    rice and Sicilian butter, 118
APPLE(S)
    cider and parsnips, chicken stew with, 24
    cranberry raisin chutney, roast chicken
      with, 78
    honey glaze, Cornish hens with fruit,
      walnuts, and, 108
    spinach salad with smoked chicken, walnuts,
      bacon, and, 152
APRICOTS
    in Cornish hens with fruit, walnuts, and
      honey-apple glaze, 108
    spiced chicken breasts with dried, 90
    spiced chicken legs with raisins and, 30
ARNEIS, *recommended with*
    arroz con pollo, 62
    risotto with smoked turkey, leeks, and
      mascarpone, 60
Arroz con pollo, 62
Artichoke hearts, grilled-chicken pasta salad
    with, 68
ARUGULA
    couscous salad with turkey and, 174
    and sun-dried tomato vinaigrette, penne
      with turkey, 72
Asparagus, grilled Asian Cornish hens with
    portobello mushrooms and, 120
Avgolemono sauce, chicken breasts with orzo,
    carrots, dill, and, 46

b

BACON
    spinach salad with smoked chicken, apple,
      walnuts, and, 152
    turkey with greens and, 142
Baked bone-in chicken breasts or thighs, 62
Baked Buffalo chicken wings, 96

BANDOL, ROSÉ, *recommended with*
    chicken pan bagnat, 168
    Moroccan chicken and potato salad with
      olives, 156
Beans. *See also specific types of beans*
    in spicy chicken chili, 20
BEAUJOLAIS, *recommended with*
    chicken souvlaki, 164
    grilled chicken with spicy Brazilian tomato
      and coconut sauce, 112
    groundnut stew, 22
    jerk chicken, 94
    penne with turkey, arugula, and sun-dried
      tomato vinaigrette, 72
    Russian-style chicken cutlets, 136
    spinach salad with smoked chicken, apple,
      walnuts, and bacon, 152
    turkey with bacon and greens, 142
BEER, *recommended with*
    baked Buffalo chicken wings, 96
    chicken burritos with black-bean salsa and
      pepper Jack, 160
    grilled chicken with spicy Brazilian tomato
      and coconut sauce, 112
    jerk chicken, 94
    kung pao chicken, 130
BERGERAC, *recommended with*
    chicken chasseur, 128
BLACK BEAN(S)
    chicken with rice and, 64
    salsa, chicken burritos with pepper Jack
      and, 160
    in spicy chicken chili, 20
BLUE CHEESE
    in baked Buffalo chicken wings, 96
    orecchiette with chicken, caramelized
      onions, and, 48
Boursin cheese sauce, chicken breasts
    with, 100
Brandied mushrooms, fettuccine with turkey
    and, 54
Breast, turkey, with mustard-sage crumbs, 84
BREAST(S), CHICKEN
    carving tips, 14

cooking tips, 14, 180, 181
substitutions for, 8
bone-in
    basic cooking method, 180, 181
    with Boursin cheese sauce, 100
    and cavatelli, 36
    chasseur, 128
    with creamy vegetable topping, 100
    grilled, with citrus glaze, 110
    grilled, with grapefruit glaze, 110
    spiced, with dried apricots, 90
boneless and skinless
    basic cooking method, 181
    burritos with black-bean salsa and
      pepper Jack, 160
    cashew, 130
    and eggplant Parmesan, 102
    grilled, and vegetable salad with lemon
      and pepper vinaigrette, 148
    grilled, pasta salad with artichoke
      hearts, 68
    Indian-spiced spinach and, 26
    kung pao, 130
    in massaman curry, 28
    and mushroom risotto, 58
    orecchiette with caramelized onions,
      blue cheese, and, 48
    with orzo, carrots, dill, and Avgolemono
      sauce, 46
    pad Thai, 52
    pasta shells with Brussels sprouts
      and, 70
    pecan-crusted, with mustard sauce, 124
    and potato salad with olives, Moroccan,
      156
    sautéed breasts with fennel and
      rosemary, 126
    sesame salad, 154
    souvlaki, 164
    spinach salad with apple, walnuts, bacon,
      and smoked, 152
    stir-fried, with Chinese cabbage, 132
    Vietnamese salad, 150
Broth, chicken, 10

LIME(S). *See also* Citrus
    Cornish hens with herb butter and, 106
    Cornish hens with scallion butter and, 106
    in grilled Asian Cornish hens with asparagus
        and portobello mushrooms, 120
    in Vietnamese chicken salad, 150
Linguine, in chicken pad Thai, 52
Liquors, essential, 12, 178
LIVERS, CHICKEN
    with caramelized onions and Madeira, 138
    with caramelized onions and port, 138
    with caramelized onions and sherry, 138
    with raisins and pine nuts, sautéed, 140

m

MÂCON, *recommended with*
    chicken breasts with orzo, carrots, dill, and
        Avgolemono sauce, 46
Madeira, chicken livers with caramelized onions
    and, 138
MADIRAN, *recommended with*
    chicken chasseur, 128
Maple-pepper glaze and sweet potatoes, roast
    chicken with, 80
Mascarpone, risotto with smoked turkey, leeks,
    and, 60
Massaman curry, 28
Measuring spoons, 13
MÉDOC, *recommended with*
    chicken thighs with lentils, chorizo, and red
        pepper, 38
MERLOT, *recommended with*
    arroz con pollo, 62
    chicken and cavatelli, 36
    chicken goulash, 34
    chicken with port and figs, 88
    chicken with rice and beans, 64
    Russian-style chicken cutlets, 136
MEURSAULT, *recommended with*
    chicken and cavatelli, 36
MINERVOIS, *recommended with*
    chicken stew with cider and parsnips, 24
    rustic garlic chicken, 32

Moroccan chicken-and-couscous soup, 42
Moroccan chicken and potato salad with
    olives, 156
MOZZARELLA CHEESE, in chicken and
    eggplant parmesan, 102
MUSHROOM(S)
    in chicken chasseur, 128
    and chicken risotto, 58
    fettuccine with turkey and brandied, 54
    grilled Asian Cornish hens with asparagus
        and portobello, 120
    in grilled chicken and vegetable salad with
        lemon and pepper vinaigrette, 148
MUSTARD
    about, 10
    -sage crumbs, turkey breast with, 84
    sauce, pecan-crusted chicken with, 124

n

Naan, 114
NEBBIOLO, *recommended with*
    chicken and eggplant Parmesan, 102
Noodle soup, chicken, with parsnips and dill, 40
Nut(s). *See also* Peanuts; Pine nuts; Walnut(s)
    about, 10

o

Oil, about, 11
OKRA, in groundnut stew, 22
OLIVES
    about, 11
    in chicken Provençal, 134
    in grilled Cornish hens with rice and
        Sicilian butter, 118
    Moroccan chicken and potato salad
        with, 156
    in southwestern tortilla salad, 158
ONION(S)
    caramelized
        chicken livers with Madeira and, 138
        chicken livers with port and, 138
        chicken livers with sherry and, 138

    orecchiette with chicken, blue cheese,
        and, 48
    in chicken pan bagnat, 168
ORANGE(S). See also Citrus
    -glazed chicken wings, 92
    in grilled Cornish hens with rice and Sicilian
        butter, 118
    in roast chicken with cranberry-apple-raisin
        chutney, 78
Orecchiette with chicken, caramelized onions,
    and blue cheese, 48
Oregano, and feta cheese, chicken with
    lemon, 98
Orzo, carrots, dill, and Avgolemono sauce,
    chicken breasts with, 46
Oven accuracy, 15

p

Pad Thai, chicken, 52
Pan bagnat, chicken, 168
Pan sauces, 182
Pantry ingredients, 10–12, 178
Panzanella stuffing, roast Cornish hens with, 82
Paprika, in chicken goulash, 34
PARMESAN (CHEESE)
    chicken and eggplant, 102
    sauce, turkey with walnut, 144
Parsley, about, 11
PARSNIPS
    chicken noodle soup with dill and, 40
    chicken stew with cider and, 24
Parts, cut-up chicken. *See* Cut-up chicken parts
PASTA
    chicken and cavatelli, 36
    chicken breasts with orzo, carrots, dill, and
        Avgolemono sauce, 46
    chicken pad Thai, 52
    fettuccine with turkey and brandied
        mushrooms, 54
    fusilli with spicy chicken sausage, tomato,
        and ricotta cheese, 50
    grilled-chicken pasta salad with artichoke
        hearts, 68